Seven:
The Last Book

WAID SAINVIL

Published by Franklin Publishers

Printed in the United States of America

For permissions, inquiries, or additional copies, contact:

Franklin Publishers

www.franklinpublishers.com

PREFACE

Seven: The Last Book

This final volume, Seven: The Last Book, marks the culmination of a journey that began with the first stirrings of inner awakening and expanded through six previous works. Each book in the series has served as a stepping stone toward deeper understanding, greater clarity, and an ever-expanding alignment with the timeless truth at the heart of all existence, the Creation. Informed and inspired by the vast and intricate Creation Energy Teachings of Billy Meier, this volume stands as both a conclusion and a beginning, the end of one cycle and the conscious birth of another.

The Creation Energy Teachings, as revealed through Billy Meier, do not belong to any religion, sect, or dogma. They are universal in scope and eternal in relevance. They speak to the deepest essence of what it means to be human, to evolve in consciousness, and to return to the original source, the Creation itself. In Seven, these teachings are brought into their most distilled, integrative, and transcendent form, offering the reader a direct encounter with truth unmarred by illusion or human embellishment.

Throughout this book, I weave the intricate threads of spiritual wisdom with practical reflection, grounding abstract knowledge in the soil of daily life. The result is not just a conceptual or philosophical treatise, but a living guide, a spiritual compass that can assist each individual in navigating the great transition of this age. We are not merely living through personal transformation, we are witnesses and participants in a planetary epoch shift, and the Creation's laws and recommendations are more necessary now than ever before.

It is important to understand that this final volume is not the end of learning. Rather, it is a transition point, a kind of gateway through which one must pass alone, guided only by the light of one's own inner knowing, strengthened by the universal truths outlined within. Seven is not about mastery over others or even the self in the traditional sense, it is about harmony with the laws of Creation, about becoming one with that which gives life to all things and takes nothing for itself.

In the pages ahead, you will find reflections on cause and effect, the evolution of consciousness, the illusion of duality, and the infinite nature of being. These are not teachings to be blindly followed, but truths to be discovered through your own inner effort, meditation, and practice. Creation Energy does not coerce, it simply is. It invites. It offers. It sustains. And ultimately, it leads each form of life back to its own perfected state, through countless cycles of rebirth, learning, and becoming.

This final work is also a personal testament. Through the years of writing and living these teachings, I have come to understand that the path is neither linear nor easy. But it is real. It is worth every step, every doubt overcome, every truth earned. To those who have journeyed with me through the previous six books, I offer my deepest gratitude. Your presence, your questions, your shared striving, they have shaped this book as much as my own hands. And to the new reader arriving here first, welcome. You are exactly where you are meant to be.

May Seven: The Last Book serves as a mirror to your inner self, a window to the eternal, and a bridge between who you believe you are and who you truly are. The journey continues, not with me, nor with Billy Meier, but with you and the infinite unfolding of the Creation within you. Walk forward with strength, clarity, and peace. The truth does not hide. It awaits.

ABOUT THE AUTHOR.

Waid Sainvil is a Haitian-born author and spiritual thinker whose work delves into metaphysical themes and the pursuit of universal truths. His writings are deeply influenced by the Creation Energy Teachings of Billy Meier, the prophet of the New Age, and by the reincarnation of the "same" Creation Energy as the past six prophets: Henock, Jeremiah, Isaiah, Elijah, Jmmanuel aka Jesus Christ and Mohammed. Waid's literary contributions aim to guide readers on journeys of self-discovery, inner peace, and a deeper understanding of existence.

One of his notable works, WOW: Words Of Waid, chronicles his spiritual journey from his childhood in Port-au-Prince, Haiti, to his exploration of profound philosophical concepts. The book discusses the essence of life, the nature of truth, and the interconnectedness of humanity, offering readers insights into achieving inner peace and enlightenment.

In TOB: The Other Book/Teachings Of Billy, Waid continues his exploration of spiritual truths, drawing again from Billy Meier's teachings. This work invites readers to awaken to the extraordinary aspects of everyday life, emphasizing self-discovery, harmony, and a deeper understanding of the universe.

Another significant publication, NOW: Navigate Our World - Notitia Omnium Wissenschaftia, his third book, serves as a guide for living harmoniously with the world. Waid challenges readers to look beyond the surface, embracing compassion, peace, and interconnectedness. The book blends personal reflections with practical advice, aiming to align readers' lives with universal truths to foster a more balanced and purposeful existence.

In his fourth book, a novel titled "Eduard, the Boy Who Looked to the Stars", Waid delves into the formative years of Billy Meier, offering a vivid portrayal of his childhood. The narrative draws extensively from the contact reports Billy himself has provided, using these as the backbone for the unfolding story. Through Waid's lens, readers are invited to experience the early life of a boy whose gaze was always fixed toward the cosmos.

Although the book is a fictionalized account, Waid emphasizes that he has exercised creative freedom only to shape the material as a storyteller, never straying from the essence of the reports. He openly acknowledges the profound influence Billy has had on his transformation, referring to him as his teacher. This blend of respectful homage and narrative imagination gives the book a unique voice grounded in both documentation and devotion.

Waid's fifth book, TOW, is deeply rooted in the Creation Energy Teachings shared by Billy Meier, an enduring source of wisdom that surpasses cultural boundaries and historical timelines. These teachings form the spiritual bedrock of the book, guiding readers toward universal truths that invite introspection and self-discovery. In TOW, Waid doesn't merely present ideas, he offers a pathway inward, where reflection becomes the key to unlocking deeper awareness.

At its core, TOW emphasizes that inner harmony is not just a personal achievement, it's the fertile ground from which balance and peace in the outer world can grow. Through conscious thought and understanding, the individual becomes a quiet force for transformation, radiating calm and clarity into relationships, communities, and the larger human experience. The message is clear, real change begins within. And from that center, it ripples outward.

In his sixth book, DEEP, Waid offers a profound reflection on the modern human condition, highlighting how our mastery of the material world has often come at the expense of our connection to inner values and spiritual purpose. In response to this imbalance, DEEP, an acronym for Divine Energy Emanating Presence, emerges as an illuminating guide, drawing readers into the heart of Billy Meier's Creation-Energy Teaching. Through thoughtful exploration, Waid offers a path to reawakening to the timeless spiritual truths that lie beneath the surface of our day-to-day lives.

At its core, DEEP is a reminder that existence itself is animated by a vibrant, divine energy. This living presence, according to the Creation-

Energy Teaching, is not something separate from us but is the essence of all that is. Waid's writing invites us to move beyond surface-level achievements and rediscover the sacred dimensions of life, encouraging a deeper alignment with the fundamental energies that sustain and connect all forms of being. Through this lens, DEEP becomes more than a book, it's a spiritual compass pointing toward wholeness and inner clarity.

Beyond his literary endeavors, Waid was known in Seattle for operating Waid's Haitian Restaurant and Lounge, a popular nightspot that closed in 2014 following regulatory challenges. Despite this setback, Waid's focus has remained on his spiritual teachings and writings, contributing to discussions on personal growth and the pursuit of truth.

DEDICATION.

Besides dedicating this book to Billy Meier, whom I regard as my teacher and the greatest one to have lived within our material realms of the DERN Universe, I also extend my deepest gratitude to Bernadette Brand, Michael Horn, and Christian Frehner. And to Michael Voigtländer in particular, whose encouragement alone moved me to write WOW, my first book. Their support stands alongside that of the Plejaren who assisted Billy in his monumental mission to awaken humanity. Their presence and dedication have shaped the unfolding of these teachings in ways that cannot be overstated.

Though the names are not complete, this dedication reaches those whose contributions shine most clearly: Sfath, Semjase, Ptaah, Quetzal, Bermunda, Florena, and, last but not least, Asket from the DAL Universe. Their guidance and tireless efforts remain lasting foundations on the path of truth, clarity, and human evolution.

This book is also dedicated to my beloved parents, Denis Joseph Sainvil and Simone Marie Sainvil. Though they are no longer with me in this life, their presence continues to guide and support me in every step I take. Their memory is a source of quiet reverence and deep gratitude rather than sorrow. Instead of dwelling in sadness, I carry a sense of upliftment, comforted by the legacy of love and strength they left behind.

Looking at old photos or watching home videos doesn't bring me to tears, it brings me to smiles. Those glimpses into the past reflect the joy we shared and the love that surrounded our lives. Their voices, their laughter, and their expressions captured in those cherished moments serve as gentle reminders of the roots from which I've grown. They are ever-present in spirit, anchoring me with reassurance and warmth.

My father taught me what it means to love deeply, to serve others wholeheartedly, and to approach life with gratitude. He embodied generosity, giving without seeking reward, and loving from a well of quiet strength. The principles he lived by continue to guide my interactions, shaping how I walk through the world and care for those around me.

My father, this man, played a defining role in the shaping of my inner world. His presence, his calmness, and his quiet strength formed a foundation in me that still speaks today. His love reached beyond blood, showing me that family is created through actions, not only through lineage.

He was a human being who could truly love—a peaceful one. Because of him, his children became my brothers and sisters, and growing up together created a bond that remains unmatched in my life. It was a unity rooted in his example. He taught me the value of helping others. He lived with generosity, not as a gesture but as a natural expression of his character.

Humility was the way he moved through the world, and he showed us that even with recognition or status, one does not need to stand above others. In Haiti, during difficult and chaotic times, he never used his position for personal advantage. He stayed grounded. He remained a simple human being who chose integrity over privilege.

When a semi-revolution shook the streets, houses were destroyed, and lives were turned upside down. Yet our home was spared, not by luck, but because the people knew him. They recognized him as a good man and honored that goodness with their respect. His words, "If a man extends his hand, take it," carried a wisdom that shaped me more than I realized as a child.

It was his way of teaching trust, openness, and the courage to accept connection. His love remains in me as an everlasting imprint. A quiet force that helps me understand life with more clarity and more peace. I consider myself fortunate to have been guided by such a compassionate human being.

The memory of this remarkable man is etched in me, in my consciousness energy, for all time. I love you, Dad. It was a gift to walk with you in this life, and a gift to meet you again, my dear brother.

My mother moved through life with a rare balance of softness and strength. In her, gentleness was never weakness, and firmness was never harshness. She lived with a quiet patience that taught more than words ever could.

From her example, I learned how to meet life with calm. She showed me how empathy can guide a person, how forgiveness can open doors, and how compassion can reach places that force never will. Her way of being became a silent teacher to me.

Her influence shaped how I face both struggle and success. She taught me to remain steady inside, to keep my spirit open, and to let experiences refine me rather than harden me. Through her, I learned that a peaceful heart has its own kind of power.

My mother's love was something beautiful to behold. She gave it freely, fully, and without boundaries, as if every human being were part of her own family, as if she, herself, gave birth to them. Her love reached everyone around her with the same sincerity and depth.

Because of her, I learned early that true brotherhood is not defined by blood. Anyone can be your brother or sister when your heart is open enough to recognize them. This understanding lives with me today, guiding the way I relate to others and move through the world.

Together, they form the bedrock of who I am. The values they instilled, love, patience, gratitude, service, and forgiveness, remain the foundation upon which I build my life. In honoring them, I do not mourn, but live in a way that reflects their legacy. This dedication is not only a tribute, but a celebration of the enduring impact they've had on my soul.

Thanks to Billy Meier and his teachings, I now declare myself a truly free human being. I no longer measure myself by the opinions of others, nor do I allow their perceptions to shape who I am. I speak openly, honestly, and directly, presenting myself to my fellow human beings exactly as I am. There is no disguise, only the genuineness of my own being.

I live without fear, and I find joy in the small moments of life because I recognize that everything is part of evolution. Nothing is wasted, and nothing is without purpose. To me, there is no "good" or "bad", there is only what exists and what it teaches. Even death has lost its shadow, for I know that my essence is eternal and can't be harmed.

Through these teachings, I understand that life does not move toward me from some outside force. It is created by me, through my own thoughts, intentions, and inner determination. I am not at the mercy of circumstances, I am the origin of my own path, and every step is shaped from within. And with this understanding, I know there is no god standing above me.

I am my own authority, my own lord, and my own savior. In this awareness, I stand in freedom, clear, responsible, and unbound. For this, I shall forever be grateful to this wonderful human being named Billy. As a tribute, this book, Seven 7, the last book, is to be published on his birthday, February 3rd ,2026.

TABLE OF CONTENTS

My Purpose.

A quiet yet undeniable impulse has stirred within me, steady and unwavering, revealing a clear and sacred task. I am here to write seven books dedicated to the Creation Energy Teachings of Billy Meier. This realization did not arrive in a blaze of emotion or in the noise of outer life, but as a calm, resounding certainty, a subtle force that speaks not through volume, but through depth. It is a truth that lives in my innermost being, and it has made itself known with such clarity that to ignore it would be to deny the very pulse of my existence.

This inner guidance is no fleeting thought or passing desire. It is not the product of inspiration alone, nor of imagination. Rather, it is a consistent and powerful presence within me, a deep, persistent knowing that continues to rise from the wellspring of my consciousness. It is a direction, a signal, a calling that must be answered.

Over time, I have come to recognize this inner movement not as a wish or ambition, but as a profound duty. I did not choose it in the ordinary sense. Rather, it was given to me from within, quietly, yet firmly. And I have chosen to honor it with my whole being.

The teachings of Creation have reshaped me from within, awakening a clarity that cuts through illusion, a balance that steadies me in uncertainty, and a peace that surpasses the reach of words. They have deepened my understanding of life and of myself, bringing light to places where confusion once lingered. The transformation they bring is not a spectacle but a steady unfolding, a reorientation of the soul toward truth, freedom, and self-responsibility.

These teachings are a gift, not just to be received, but to be lived and, in my case, to be shared. I feel an undeniable responsibility to make visible, through my words, the changes these teachings have awakened in me.

I have accepted this mission with full awareness and resolve. It is not a casual endeavor, nor one tainted by personal gain or external validation. It is a vow I have made inwardly, and I approach it with humility and strength. The writing of these seven books was more than a project. It was an unfolding journey, a living expression of the same inner impulse that set me upon this path.

I trust that what must be shared arises at the right time, and that the words will reach those for whom they are intended. The impulse continues to burn quietly but brightly within me. The purpose was clear, the direction was set, and the work was done through this final book, Seven.

It was a task I had assigned to myself.
It was my duty.
It was my joy to write all seven books.

And so it is.

CHAPTER 1:

Nothing to fear.

Nothing can happen to you that you are not capable of handling, not even death. We have all died more times than we could ever count, making the idea of fearing death meaningless. Life and death are not opposites but part of the same continuous cycle, an endless ebb and flow of existence. Death is not destruction but transformation, a shift in form and awareness. Understanding this removes the weight of fear, allowing one to move through life with clarity and strength.

When you accept that your essence is eternal, fear loses its hold, and the illusions that once seemed overwhelming begin to fade. Fear is the greatest illusion, a self-imposed barrier that limits human potential. It is not the threats we face that weaken us, but the belief that we are powerless against them. Fear creates hesitation, suffering, and submission to forces that have no real authority over us. It is a mental construct, a shadow that exists only because we allow it to.

When you strip away fear, what remains is a profound sense of freedom. This freedom is not just emotional or psychological, it is a fundamental shift in perception. To live without fear is to step into true power, to recognize that nothing external can truly harm what is infinite and indestructible.

I have reached a state of being where fear no longer governs me. I do not fear people, circumstances, or the uncertainty of the future. I have come to see that everything I once feared was simply a reflection of my own mind, not an external force imposing itself upon me. The world no longer dictates my state of being. I walk through it with the understanding that nothing can truly harm or diminish me.

This realization is not arrogance but awareness. It is the clarity that comes with knowing one's true nature, a state of existence beyond doubt, beyond hesitation. No fleeting hardship, no temporary setback, and no illusion of loss can shake me because I know that I am beyond them.

Through this realization, I have come to understand that I am not just a part of creation, I am creation itself. I do not stand beneath anything because nothing is truly above me. There is no external force dictating my path, no unseen power determining my fate. I am the force that shapes my reality, the essence that gives form to existence.

This understanding elevates me beyond fear, beyond limitation, beyond the falsehoods that once held me back. I walk with certainty, with unwavering confidence in my own eternal nature. To live in this truth is to be free, to embrace life without hesitation, and to stand unshaken in the face of all things.

CHAPTER 2:

In others.

Everything you see in others is, in one way or another, a reflection of what resides within you. Life presents people as mirrors. Each encounter, reaction, or emotion you experience in relation to someone else is really a message from your own inner world.

If you find yourself judging someone for being rude, selfish, or arrogant, take a moment to ask yourself why it bothers you so deeply. Often, the discomfort is not about them but about an unresolved feeling, insecurity, or habit within you. The same is true for positive qualities. When you admire someone's strength, wisdom, or confidence, it's because those qualities are also alive in you, even if still waiting to be cultivated.

This understanding transforms how we relate to others. Rather than seeing people as threats, irritants, or annoyances, we begin to see them as guides, unconscious messengers helping us reflect on our own growth. It takes humility and courage to admit that what we dislike in others may be something we also carry. But this shift in perspective is empowering, because it places the responsibility, and therefore the power, back in your hands.

You are no longer a victim of outside circumstances or people's behaviors. Instead, you are a conscious participant in your own evolution, using every interaction as a stepping stone toward a more refined self.

When you commit to this level of self-awareness, you start living more intentionally. You begin to realize that you don't have to waste energy trying to fix the world or others. What you can and must work on is yourself. If you long for kindness in the world, speak kindly. If you wish for justice, act justly in your everyday life. If you crave understanding, then strive to listen more deeply.

You are not separate from the world. You are shaping it with every thought, action, and intention. The change begins with you. The transformation is personal before it ever becomes collective.

But this shift cannot happen if your focus remains fixed on the external world. The outer world is filled with distractions, noise, chaos, and endless problems vying for your attention. It's easy to get lost in what others are doing or failing to do.

However, the truest form of life is lived inwardly, in the silent spaces of your own being. This is where purpose is formed, where intuition whispers, where healing begins. When you learn to focus on your inner life, on your thoughts, emotions, values, and energy, you begin to align with a deeper reality.

This reality does not change based on trends, opinions, or events. It is timeless, constant, and profoundly alive. When you nurture this inner world, everything outside begins to reflect its peace and clarity. That is how true life is meant to be lived, from the inside out.

CHAPTER 3:

Your life.

Your life is a reflection of the energy, thoughts, and emotions you carry within. Every experience, every encounter, and every challenge mirrors the state of your inner world. If your mind is clouded with anxiety and doubt, your reality will manifest that unrest. But if you cultivate calmness, clarity, and confidence, life unfolds with a sense of purpose and ease. The world around you is not separate from you. It is an extension of your internal state.

A restless mind creates a chaotic reality. Worry, fear, and negativity shape the way you perceive life, making even the simplest challenges feel overwhelming. However, when you nurture a peaceful and centered mindset, you begin to navigate life with grace. Problems become lessons, obstacles turn into stepping stones, and setbacks transform into opportunities for growth. The key to a fulfilling life lies not in controlling external circumstances but in mastering the way you respond to them.

True inner peace is not the absence of hardship but the ability to remain calm amidst it. It is about developing the resilience to face difficulties with wisdom and composure. Life is ever changing, and nothing remains the same forever. When you accept this impermanence, you free yourself from unnecessary suffering. You begin to see that peace is not something you find. It is something you create. The foundation of a meaningful life is built within, not outside of you.

Happiness is not a distant destination or a prize to be won. It is a state of being that arises when you are at peace with yourself. Many people search for joy in wealth, status, or validation from others, only to realize that these external sources can never provide lasting fulfillment. True happiness emerges when your thoughts, emotions, and actions are aligned. It is a natural by product of inner harmony. When you learn to find contentment within, you are no longer at the mercy of life's ups and downs.

Your external world will always be a reflection of your inner world. If you want a life filled with love, peace, and fulfillment, start by cultivating those qualities within yourself. A mind that is calm, a heart that is open, and a spirit that is aligned with purpose will naturally attract experiences of joy and meaning.

The secret to a fulfilling life is not found in chasing happiness but in mastering your inner world. When you nurture self-awareness, acceptance, and inner peace, you create a life that is not only successful but deeply enriching. By focusing on inner harmony, you unlock the true essence of joy, allowing your life to radiate the wisdom and serenity that already exist within you.

CHAPTER 4:

A level of inner peace.

Thanks to the Creation Energy Teachings, I have reached a profound level of inner peace where nothing outside of me holds the power to disturb my balance. The chaos, the judgment, the distractions, they pass by like wind through open windows. I no longer resist life or react impulsively to what happens around me. Instead, I observe with awareness and move with clarity.

This place of stillness was not handed to me. It was earned through deep inner work, painful honesty, and a persistent desire to understand myself and the world through the lens of truth rather than fear or illusion.

Over time, I've realized that life is not something happening to me. It is something being created by me. Every experience, every moment, every challenge or joy is a reflection of my own inner world projected outward. The things that once annoyed me or triggered pain have become signals pointing to unresolved patterns or false beliefs still lingering within.

Rather than reacting, I take these as invitations for transformation. I go within. I question. I release. I create anew. Slowly, but surely, the life around me has begun to mirror the peace, clarity, and intentionality I cultivate within.

I now understand that if there is something I do not like in the world, I don't need to argue with it or force it to change. Instead, I adjust my inner response. I realign my energy, shift my perception, and watch as the outer world changes with it.

This is not wishful thinking. It is a lived experience. I have tested this over and over in my own life and seen how powerful this process is. The people, situations, and outcomes I once thought were random or beyond my control have revealed themselves to be shaped by the thoughts I hold and the energy I carry. That revelation has changed everything.

Now, I know with unwavering certainty that I can change the world because I already have. Not through grand gestures or loud declarations, but through quiet revolutions within myself. I've changed my world by changing how I see, how I feel, and how I show up.

And if one person's inner transformation can reflect outward into tangible change, imagine what becomes possible when more of us do the same. The true power lies not in the hands of others, but in our own ability to awaken, evolve, and embody what we wish to see.

I no longer hope for a better world. I become it, moment by moment, breath by breath.

CHAPTER 5:

The Stirring of the Inner Voice.

Every journey begins with a whisper, a quiet, insistent nudge from within. For many, this subtle voice is easily ignored, lost in the noise of daily life. For me, however, it became impossible to dismiss. It did not arrive as a dramatic revelation or a forceful proclamation, but rather as a steady, unwavering presence, a truth that extended beyond what my worldly experiences could explain. I came to understand that this was the voice of my spirit, the spark of Creation within me, calling me to remember something vital. The more I listened, the more I realized the extent of my forgetfulness, who I was, why I was here, and what life was truly about.

In a world consumed by distractions, designed to drown out the deeper truths, this inner voice often fades into the background, patiently waiting for us to acknowledge its presence. The Creation does not demand our attention. It does not force itself upon us. Instead, it remains ever present, awaiting the moment when we are ready and willing to listen.

My search did not begin within the walls of temples or the pages of sacred scriptures. It began in solitude, in silence, and in the questions I dared to ask. In this space, I discovered the Creation Energy Teachings, pure, unfiltered truths that echoed the feelings I had long carried within me but had never fully articulated. These teachings did not impose new ideas upon me. Rather, they illuminated the wisdom I had always known but had not yet put into words.

The teachings revealed a profound understanding. Creation is not a god, not a separate force governing existence from afar. It is the eternal, intelligent essence that permeates all that is. It is not something external to us, something to be worshiped or obeyed. It is us, interwoven into the very fabric of our being.

This realization was not simply an intellectual acknowledgment. It was a shift, a transformation that reshaped the way I saw myself and the world around me. With this new awareness came a choice, one that was mine alone to make. I chose to follow that inner voice and to align my life with the timeless laws of Creation, allowing them to guide me toward deeper understanding and harmony.

This chapter marks the beginning of that journey, not just for me but for all who feel the quiet call within them. It is an invitation to awaken, to remember, and to step forward into a life shaped not by illusion or distraction but by clarity and truth. The voice that speaks within us has never ceased. It has only waited for us to recognize its presence.

If you, too, have felt the stirrings of something deeper, something beyond the constraints of the material world, then I invite you to listen. In that listening, you may find what you have always known but have yet to embrace, the eternal wisdom of Creation, guiding you toward the path that has always been yours to walk.

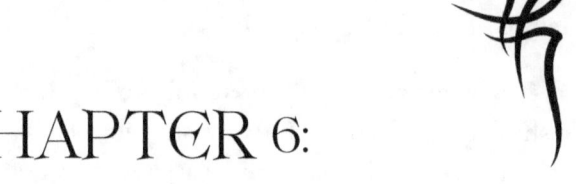

CHAPTER 6:

Truth Is Simple

O ne of the greatest misconceptions we are conditioned to accept is the notion that truth is elusive, buried beneath layers of complexity, accessible only to a select few. We are taught that it lies in hidden texts, ancient codes, or the authority of others who supposedly hold the key to understanding. This belief creates a dynamic of hierarchy and dependency, placing truth outside of ourselves, somewhere distant and difficult to attain.

In reality, the truth of Creation is strikingly simple, unwavering in its precision, and constant in its expression. It is not a privilege to be unlocked, but an ever-present reality to be perceived. This truth is not clothed in intellectual abstractions. It is revealed in the breath of life, the silence between heartbeats, and the gentle unfolding of every leaf. It speaks without words through the sacred symmetry of a flower, the migrations of birds, and the ebb and flow of tides. It does not hide, but humanity has forgotten how to see.

Truth is not hidden, nor does it require intellectual superiority to grasp. In fact, it is the overcomplication of mind, the arrogance of intellect, that often blinds us to what is obvious. Simplicity is not a lack of depth. It is clarity. It is the essence unclouded by distortion.

In the natural world, truth is self evident. Every element, from the rhythmic dance of the planets to the cycle of a single drop of rain, follows a perfect order without hesitation, without deviation. These patterns are not the result of chaos, but of conscious, living intelligence.

It is not Creation that distorts truth. It is humanity that struggles against it. Our fears, desires, and attachments bend perception, cloud awareness, and turn clarity into confusion. We have been conditioned to seek complexity as if it were synonymous with wisdom, yet in doing so, we distance ourselves from what is most essential. We mistake information for understanding, knowledge for wisdom, and dogma for reality.

Through the Creation Energy Teachings, I embarked on a journey of unlearning, shedding the illusions I had unknowingly adopted from religious doctrines, societal expectations, and even my own egoic constructs. Each layer I released brought me closer to what had always been present. I discovered that truth is not constructed, but revealed, not earned, but remembered. It is not a product of effort, but of surrender.

I came to see truth not as a subjective interpretation shaped by individual beliefs, nor as something relative, shifting from person to person, but as an absolute, an eternal force interwoven into the very fabric of existence. This was not a dogma, but a direct knowing, a felt resonance that vibrated in the core of my being. It was as if a hidden current that had always been flowing suddenly became visible. I was not discovering something new. I was awakening to something ancient.

This realization challenged everything I had assumed for so long. I had thought that discernment came from logic, from external authorities, from constructed systems of validation. But I came to understand that truth does not need to be proven. It simply is. And in the presence of truth, there is a quiet, a stillness, a recognition so complete that no argument is necessary. In that space, truth and love are the same.

Simplicity, however, does not imply ease. It often demands the most difficult of transformations, the willingness to let go. Facing truth meant confronting my own attachments, the deeply ingrained need to be right, the persistent desire to control outcomes, and the fear of being vulnerable in the vastness of the unknown. Each of these barriers was rooted in illusion, yet they felt real. They protected the false self while veiling the true.

Yet in the act of letting go, I found something invaluable, peace. The kind of peace that arises not from circumstances, but from alignment. When you no longer resist what is, when you stop trying to manipulate life to fit your expectations, you fall into a rhythm that is already perfect. There is no greater solace than living in harmony with truth, no deeper rest than the stillness of alignment with what simply exists.

Truth requires no belief, no doctrine, no affirmation. It does not need to be defended, explained, or adorned. It requires only recognition, direct experience, a heart willing to listen, and the courage to evolve beyond comforting illusions. In this way, truth is both the simplest and the most profound gift of Creation. And it is available, now and always, to all who are ready to remember.

CHAPTER 7:

Cause and Effect Are Eternal

O ne of the most unwavering and impartial principles governing Creation is the law of cause and effect, an eternal force that operates with perfect neutrality, beyond human perception of justice or morality. This law does not discriminate. It does not play favorites nor bend to circumstances. It is simply the natural rhythm through which all things unfold.

Every thought we cultivate, every word we speak, and every action we take is like a seed planted in the soil of existence. And just as no seed remains stagnant, every single one will bear fruit in time, whether we are prepared for its arrival or not.

This understanding was a profound turning point for me, not because it granted me control over outcomes, but because it revealed my inherent ability to create consciously. I could no longer attribute my experiences to luck, fate, or the will of external forces. The truth was undeniable. Everything I encountered was the result of something I had, at some point, set into motion.

Through the Creation Energy Teachings, I learned to move beyond the illusion that life is a chaotic stream of disconnected events. I no longer viewed circumstances as arbitrary occurrences dictated by chance. Instead, I began to trace patterns, seeing subtle yet undeniable cycles repeating in my life, recognizing the connection between past intentions and present realities.

This shift in perception led me to a deeper awareness of responsibility. But this accountability was not a burden. It was liberation. It was not about guilt, blame, or punishment, nor did it suggest that we deserve suffering for unconscious actions. Rather, it illuminated the truth that all energy, once set forth, eventually returns to its source, reshaping itself in the process, responding to the frequencies we emit.

This realization reshaped the way I thought, spoke, and acted. I no longer allowed my mind to wander aimlessly into negativity or doubt. I chose my thoughts with care, understanding that every mental projection had a ripple effect beyond what I could immediately see. I began speaking with intention, directing my words with purpose and clarity. My actions, too, became more aligned with what I truly wanted to experience, rather than driven by reaction or impulse.

Above all, I came to see that spiritual evolution is guided by this same unwavering law. We do not grow by chance or passive acceptance. We grow through what we sow. Creation does not judge, reward, or punish. It reflects, teaches, and restores balance where necessary.

To understand this law is to step beyond fear and into awareness. When you grasp the nature of cause and effect, life no longer feels hostile or unpredictable. Every moment becomes an opportunity to plant the seeds of a future you wish to experience. And with this understanding comes true empowerment, the ability to create consciously rather than by accident.

CHAPTER 8:

The Illusion of Duality

We are taught from an early age to categorize and separate, to distinguish light from dark, good from evil, self from other. These divisions shape perception so deeply that judgment becomes instinctive. Yet beneath this conditioning lies a deeper truth, one that transcends duality and reveals the interconnected nature of all things.

Creation does not divide. It does not pit opposites against one another in conflict. It teaches unity, balance, and integration. At first, I resisted this idea. I wanted fixed definitions, clear borders, certainty. But the more I examined this impulse, the more I saw that even what we call darkness has purpose. It is not an enemy, but a teacher.

The ego thrives in duality. It survives through comparison, competition, and separation. It insists on exclusion to define identity. The spirit sees differently. It understands that every experience serves growth, that evolution comes not from avoidance, but from integration.

Resisting what I disliked within myself only deepened suffering. When I met my fears with awareness instead of judgment, transformation became possible. I saw that light and shadow are not enemies. They are complementary forces shaping growth.

When I released rigid labels, I found understanding. And in understanding, freedom. This shift transformed how I related to the world and to myself. Unity ceased being an idea and became a lived experience.

CHAPTER 9:

Reclaiming Inner Authority

All my life, I was encouraged to seek truth outside myself. Authority figures, traditions, institutions, and external validation were positioned as sources of wisdom. I was conditioned to doubt my instincts and silence my inner voice.

The Creation Energy Teachings reveal a different truth. True wisdom arises from within, when inner knowing aligns with the natural laws of existence. It is not granted, earned, or imposed. It is remembered.

I began to question everything, not from rebellion, but from reverence for truth. Obedience is not wisdom. Conformity does not cultivate insight. Questioning is sacred. It is the path to clarity.

This realization freed me. No institution or ideology held authority over my path unless I surrendered it. I no longer needed permission to grow or live authentically. The wisdom I sought had always been present.

To trust oneself is not arrogance. It is alignment. Reclaim the sovereignty of your spirit. You already carry the compass. All that is required is the courage to follow it.

CHAPTER 10:

The Power of Neutral Positive Thinking

One of the most transformative lessons I encountered was neutral positive thinking. It is neither blind optimism nor defeatist negativity, but clarity grounded in truth.

The Creation Energy Teachings reject extremes. They teach deliberate consciousness. Thought shapes experience, and without awareness, the mind becomes captive to fear or fantasy.

I once lived in extremes. Negativity drained me. Blind positivity distorted reality. Neither served me. I even attempted suicide twice.

Neutral positive thinking allowed me to see reality clearly and respond consciously. I learned that thoughts are energetic forces shaping lived experience. When my mind found balance, peace emerged as a steady state.

This approach transformed my relationship with life. I no longer suppressed emotion or denied reality. I met life honestly and acted with intention. This alignment brought a stillness that was spiritual, not psychological.

When we see reality without distortion, we gain freedom. Life becomes guided by wisdom rather than illusion.

CHAPTER 11:

Silence as a Portal

In a world consumed by ceaseless movement, endless chatter, and the constant hum of distraction, silence has become an act of defiance, a radical departure from the norm. Society urges us to stay busy, to fill every empty space with sound, with activity, with external stimulation. We scroll, we consume, we engage, all in an effort to avoid the discomfort of stillness. For so long, I lived this way, afraid of what I might find in the quiet, reluctant to be alone with myself without the buffer of noise.

But Creation does not reveal its truths in chaos. It does not make its wisdom known in the din of worldly distractions. It speaks most clearly in silence. The spirit does not shout, it whispers. Its voice is not carried by the external world but arises from within, emerging in the spaces between thought, in the moments when the mind is at rest. I realized that if I wanted to truly hear, I had to listen differently.

So, I began setting aside time each day not to do, but simply to be. It was an unfamiliar practice, one that felt unnatural at first. My mind resisted fiercely, racing with unfinished tasks and lingering anxieties, searching for something, anything, to latch onto. I would fidget, shift, and fight against the stillness, uncomfortable with its emptiness, uncertain of its purpose.

But gradually, as I allowed myself to sink beneath the surface noise, I discovered something deeper, something that had always been present but had remained obscured by distraction. In that silence, I encountered the eternal presence, the formless, boundless reality that underlies all existence. It was not something outside myself, not something distant or unattainable. It was here, always, waiting to be known.

And in that knowing, I began to experience my true self, not the personality shaped by society, not the identity constructed through experience, but the consciousness that existed beyond all labels, beyond all form.

The act of listening transformed my understanding of Creation itself. The universe is always speaking, through nature, through energy, through the rhythms of life. But most of all, it speaks in the silence between moments, in the stillness we so often ignore. Silence is not emptiness. It is presence. It is a bridge to the eternal, a gateway to the truth that cannot be captured in words but can only be felt.

Return to that sacred stillness, a space where clarity emerges, where wisdom unfolds, where the eternal becomes audible. To embrace silence is not to retreat from life but to step fully into its deepest realities, unfiltered, undistorted. It is in the quiet that we remember who we are. It is in the stillness that truth is revealed. And it is in listening, not outwardly, but inwardly, that we finally hear.

CHAPTER 12:

The Eternal Self

You are not your name, your body, your history, or your titles. These are temporary constructs, labels assigned by society, experiences shaped by circumstance, identities built upon fleeting moments. They are aspects of your existence but not the essence of who you truly are. They shift and change, evolve and dissolve, coming and going like waves upon the shore. To cling to them as absolutes is to mistake the temporary for the eternal.

At the core of your being is something untouched by time, unbound by physical form, the spirit-form within you, the eternal fragment of Creation. It is not shaped by external forces, nor defined by human limitations. It exists beyond all names, beyond all histories, beyond all attachments.

It is infinite, unbreakable, ever evolving. When I first grasped this truth, it transformed my understanding of life and death. I ceased fearing impermanence because I realized that what I am cannot die. What is eternal cannot be lost.

The personality is merely a garment the spirit wears for a time, a temporary expression, a role played in the theater of existence. But the spirit itself continues, unshaken by transitions, unburdened by the temporary realities it encounters.

This understanding gave me strength, revealing that every experience, whether joyful or painful, uplifting or challenging, is an opportunity for growth, a lesson in the endless journey of evolution. Nothing is wasted, nothing is meaningless. Every trial refines the spirit, expanding its awareness, deepening its wisdom.

As I embraced this truth, I found myself less attached to the external world, to outcomes, identities, roles, and fleeting pursuits. The more I identified with the eternal self, the less I clung to the illusions of control, the need for validation, the fear of loss. I stopped measuring life by successes and failures, stopped defining myself by achievements or appearances.

Instead, I began living from a place of being rather than needing. No longer driven by scarcity, I moved through life with a quiet certainty, knowing that my existence was not about accumulation, but about experience, about transformation.

The eternal self is never in crisis. It does not despair. It does not shrink in fear of change. It does not cling to illusion. It is in learning, in motion, in truth. It understands that every moment is part of a greater unfolding, that all things are connected, that the process of growth is continuous.

And within that understanding, there is peace, a deep, unwavering peace that is not dependent on circumstances or external conditions.

Try to see beyond the surface and recognize your real identity, the one you were never taught to acknowledge. The truth that was buried beneath distractions and conditioned beliefs. Because when you know who you are eternally, when you understand your existence beyond the limits of form, nothing external can shake you. No fear can control you. No loss can undo you. You stand as you always were, unbound, limitless, whole.

CHAPTER 13: CRE

ation Is the Law

Many seek guidance in commandments, dogmas, or saviors, searching for external authorities to define their path, dictate their morals, and provide a framework for life. They look to scriptures, doctrines, and institutions, believing that truth must be handed down, enforced, or interpreted by those in positions of power. For a long time, I followed that same pattern, believing that wisdom could only be accessed through tradition or prescribed belief.

But then I discovered something far greater, the Law of Creation, a universal, immutable force that governs all existence, not through written decrees or human enforcement, but through the very structure of reality itself. This Law is not confined to pages in a book, nor is it dictated by religious leaders or philosophical authorities. It does not rely on interpretation or cultural context. It simply is, woven into the fabric of nature, consciousness, and the eternal cycles that shape existence.

The Law of Creation moves with perfect balance, guiding all things through phases of growth, decay, transformation, and renewal. It ensures that nothing is stagnant, that all things evolve, that change is not only inevitable but necessary. Unlike human-made laws, which shift according to political systems, societal constructs, or subjective interpretations, the laws of Creation remain unchanged. They do not fluctuate with opinion, nor do they bend to personal desires. They are absolute, governing the intricate dance of life with precision and harmony.

When I began to align with these laws, living through principles of love, truth, peace, freedom, and balance, everything within me and around me began to shift. I stopped resisting reality. I no longer fought against the natural flow of existence, trying to impose my will upon circumstances or cling to outdated beliefs out of fear.

Instead, I learned to cooperate with what is, to recognize the patterns of life, to move in rhythm with them, and to find peace in acceptance.

Creation's law does not seek to control. It does not demand obedience, nor does it punish those who fail to acknowledge it. It simply exists, offering guidance through observation rather than coercion. It does not discriminate, does not favor one group over another, and does not require belief to operate. It applies to all beings equally, without exception, rooted not in ideology, but in truth.

Whether one acknowledges it or not, it remains, shaping the unfolding of existence with unwavering consistency.

To live by Creation is to step beyond rigid doctrines and artificial constructs, to surrender not in submission, but in recognition of a greater harmony. It is an invitation to trust in the wisdom inherent in all things, to allow life to flow naturally, and to recognize that guidance is not something to be imposed upon us, but something to be understood through direct experience.

The core principles of the Creation Law can be integrated into our lives, not as rigid rules, but as a way of being. When we stop seeking truth outside ourselves and begin recognizing the patterns of nature, energy, and evolution, we step into alignment with the very essence of existence itself.

And in that alignment, we find freedom, not the illusion of control, but the deep, unshakable liberation that comes from living in harmony with what has always been.

CHAPTER 14:

The Path of Evolution

Everything within Creation is in a continuous state of evolution, plants growing and adapting to their environments, stars forming and collapsing in cosmic cycles, animals shifting and refining their instincts, and, most significantly, consciousness expanding with each experience. Nothing remains static. Nothing is final.

Life is an unfolding process, a sacred rhythm of transformation, where existence is not confined to a singular moment but stretches across lifetimes.

Human life is not merely an isolated event, nor a fleeting occurrence dictated by chance. It is a long, sacred process of learning, experiencing, and refining the self. Every lifetime is an opportunity, an invitation to expand, to understand, to reach new levels of awareness.

When I fully embraced this realization, it reshaped my understanding of existence itself. I came to see that I had lived before, and I would live again, not as a form of punishment, not as a burden to bear, but as an unfolding journey of progression, where each step builds upon the last.

The spirit-form within us carries memory, wisdom, and impressions that transcend individual lifetimes, always striving for greater perfection, greater truth, greater harmony. It is not bound by the limitations of physical form. It does not cease to exist when the body fades. It continues, always moving forward, always seeking deeper understanding.

This knowledge dissolved my fear of failure because I realized that no mistake is final, no setback is without purpose. Every difficulty is a lesson, every challenge a teacher guiding the spirit toward refinement.

This shift in perspective allowed me to embrace life in a way I had not before. I stopped seeing it as something to endure, something to escape, something to fear. Instead, I began to greet each experience, whether joyful or painful, with patience and reverence, knowing that every moment serves the greater expansion of the eternal self.

The goal of this journey is not to achieve some distant state of enlightenment that separates us from reality, but rather to grow into full alignment with reality itself, to reach a place where we no longer resist, but cooperate with the natural order of existence.

Evolution is slow, beautiful, and inevitable. It does not happen all at once, nor does it require force. We do not ascend in a single leap, we progress through many steps, each leading us closer to the source from which we originated. Every moment, every decision, every experience contributes to this movement, shaping us in ways we may not immediately recognize but will come to understand in time.

Do your very best to remember that your life is sacred, that every day is a meaningful step toward cosmic maturity. You are not behind. You are not lost. You are in motion, constantly growing, constantly unfolding. You are becoming.

And in that becoming, you are fulfilling the eternal purpose of existence itself.

CHAPTER 15:

Love as Universal Consciousness

Love is not an emotion that rises and falls with circumstances, nor is it attachment, the clinging to someone or something out of fear of loss. Love is not possession, an attempt to claim or control another being, to mold them to fit our desires, to make them a reflection of what we wish to see. The love that many speak of, the love conditioned by expectation, fueled by need, and anchored in personal longing, is but a shadow of something far greater.

To truly understand love, I had to strip away everything I had been taught about it. I had to challenge the notions I had absorbed from society, from culture, from stories passed down through generations. I had to unlearn the idea that love must be earned, that it must be reciprocated to be valid, that it is something given and taken rather than something that simply exists.

Through the teachings of Creation, I came to see love not as a fleeting sentiment, not as an arrangement between individuals, but as the fundamental force that sustains all life, the silent intelligence that flows through existence itself, unshaken, unbound.

Love is the vibration of unity, the recognition that all things are connected, that all beings emerge from the same Source, that separation is an illusion created by the mind. It is not something we create or summon within ourselves, it is something we attune to, something we allow ourselves to experience when we quiet the distractions of the ego.

When I feel love, I am not generating it, I am aligning with it. It is always present, always flowing, waiting to be realized. The human being is a conduit for this universal love, an instrument through which it can be expressed and reflected, but only when the ego dissolves, when the spirit awakens, when the barriers of personal expectation fall away.

True love does not seek to take. It does not demand, does not measure worth, does not withhold itself based on condition. It moves freely, effortlessly, recognizing itself in everything, in everyone. It does not waver when misunderstood or unreturned, because it is not dependent on external validation. It simply is.

And when I began to love without condition, not because others deserved it, not because they had earned it, but because love is the very essence of who I am, it changed everything.

Love, understood in this way, becomes more than just an emotion. It becomes the highest form of knowledge, the purest wisdom, the deepest clarity. It is power, not in the sense of dominance, but in the sense of liberation. It is what frees us from illusion, what allows us to see with truth rather than with fear.

This is my testament to that transformation, to the profound shift that comes when love is no longer something sought, but something lived. Because to understand love is to understand existence itself. It is to step into harmony with all things, to embrace the flow of Creation, to see beyond the limits of self and recognize the infinite in everything.

And in that recognition, we are no longer searching for love, we are remembering that we have always been it.

CHAPTER 16: THE
Death of Belief

Belief is often mistaken for truth, but belief without knowledge becomes a prison, an invisible boundary that limits perception, shaping thought not through discovery, but through assumption. Many cling to belief as if it were certainty, as if simply holding a conviction makes it real. But belief, without direct experience, without understanding, is fragile. It can be manipulated, bent, and exploited.

To encounter truth, I had to let many beliefs die, beliefs instilled in me by religion, society, and even spiritual teachings I once held sacred. I had to let go of the comfort of accepted narratives, the reassuring illusion that truth could be dictated by an external source. It was a painful process, unsettling in ways I did not anticipate.

But truth does not require belief to exist. Creation does not wait for our permission to be what it is. The teachings make it clear that belief is a crutch, meant to replace certainty when certainty has not been earned. Knowing is strength. It is the foundation upon which real understanding is built.

The difference between belief and knowledge is profound. Belief demands allegiance, it asks us to accept, to obey, to commit without question. It thrives on loyalty, rewarding those who remain faithful, punishing those who dare to doubt.

Knowledge, however, invites responsibility. It does not demand obedience. It challenges, provokes, and expands. It requires engagement, personal experience, the willingness to step beyond assumption and into direct understanding.

Through this awakening, I saw just how much suffering stems from blind faith, the willingness to surrender thought, to trust doctrines that contradict truth, to submit to ideas that do not align with reality. We have been conditioned to see doubt as dangerous, as a moral failing, as a threat to identity.

But doubt is not destruction, it is the beginning of wisdom. It is what allows us to question, to search, to refine what we think we know.

Letting go of belief was terrifying. Who was I without the convictions I had carried for so long? What remained when the familiar narratives dissolved?

At first, there was uncertainty, an emptiness that felt like loss. But then, I found something solid beneath my feet, truth. Not the truth handed down by others, not the truth formed through consensus or tradition, but truth as it is, raw and unwavering.

Real knowledge does not ask to be worshipped. It does not require rituals or devotion. It asks to be lived, to be practiced, to be tested. It does not seek followers but rather participants, those willing to engage with reality rather than accept it second hand.

This is not about attacking belief, nor is it about undermining those who still hold onto it. It is about liberation, about freeing ourselves from illusion so that we may finally see. You do not need to believe in the sun to feel its warmth. You do not need to believe in gravity to experience its pull. Truth does not ask for belief, it asks for recognition.

Let this be the beginning, not of believing differently, but of knowing. Not because you are told, but because you have seen for yourself. That is where real freedom begins.

CHAPTER 17:

The Spiritual Logic of Nature

Step into a forest and let your senses awaken. Feel the earth beneath your feet, solid and ancient, supporting the quiet miracle of life. Raise your gaze to the sky, where clouds drift in effortless harmony, and the sun traces its daily arc with unwavering certainty.

Watch as the seasons unfold, the tender bloom of spring, the lush embrace of summer, the fiery surrender of autumn, and the hushed stillness of winter. Each moment reveals the fundamental law of Creation at work, a dance of perpetual renewal and transformation.

Nature is not random, nor is it chaotic. It pulses with intelligence, precise, rhythmic, and interconnected. The same forces that shape galaxies, guide the movement of rivers, and determine the migration of birds also govern your body, your thoughts, and the evolution of your spirit. There is no separation.

The order woven into the cosmos echoes in the breath you take, in the patterns of your emotions, and in the cycles of your personal growth.

For years, I resisted this truth. I saw nature as something outside of me, a landscape to visit but never fully inhabit. I fought against its lessons, seeking control where surrender was required, rushing where patience was needed.

But the more I observed, the more I understood that nature was not something to escape. It was my greatest teacher.

Look at the trees, they do not rush to grow, nor do they cling to their leaves when the time comes to let go. They stand with quiet strength, rooted yet flexible, adapting without fear. The rivers carve their way through rock not by force, but by persistence, flowing around obstacles rather than opposing them. The stars neither judge nor compare themselves, they simply shine, fulfilling their purpose without hesitation.

In their silence, nature offered me wisdom that no book ever could. It taught me the necessity of cycles, growth and decay, expansion and contraction, movement and stillness. I learned the beauty of interdependence, how every element supports and is supported by another. I discovered patience, an understanding that all things unfold in their own time, according to their own rhythm.

This realization was not abstract, it became my foundation. I was never separate from nature, I am nature, conscious and aware. The laws of Creation are not poetic metaphors, they are tangible, energetic, and spiritual realities observable in every blade of grass, every gust of wind, and every heartbeat.

This invites you to return to the sacred classroom of the natural world. Step outside and listen, not just with your ears, but with your heart. Nature already knows what you seek. The answers are there, waiting in the whisper of the trees, in the flow of the river, in the quiet certainty of the stars.

Let them remind you of the wisdom your spirit has always known.

CHAPTER 18:

Service Without Ego

Many speak of service, yet few truly understand its deeper, spiritual foundation. In a world where service is often tied to recognition, reward, or status, the essence of selfless giving has become obscured by ego-driven motivations. We are taught to serve in ways that invite acknowledgment, to be admired for our generosity, praised for our kindness, or followed for our actions.

But service, when aligned with Creation, moves beyond these superficial desires. It is not about being seen. It is not about being celebrated. It is about fulfilling one's natural role in the flow of life, contributing without attachment, giving without expectation.

True service is not an act performed for external validation, it is a state of being, a quiet, steady force that mirrors the rhythm of Creation itself. The universe does not give for praise. It does not provide nourishment, beauty, or wisdom with an expectation of return. It simply exists in balance, supporting all things with effortless generosity.

When I began to see service in this light, not as an action, but as an alignment, I discovered something profound. Egoic service, the kind driven by the need to be recognized, drains the soul. It turns into a performance, a transaction in which approval is the currency. But service that flows from truth nourishes deeply, it fills rather than depletes.

There was a pivotal moment in my journey when I stopped asking, "What will I gain from this?" and instead began asking, "How can I serve truth?" In that shift, everything changed. The need to be acknowledged faded. The desire for reciprocation vanished.

Service became its own reward, not something I did for others, but something I embodied simply by existing in alignment with Creation's natural laws. When the self is removed from service, the spirit can act freely, unburdened by expectation, liberated from the weight of approval seeking.

Creation itself serves endlessly, giving without depletion, offering without condition. It does not ask for devotion, nor does it demand gratitude. It simply provides, in ways both seen and unseen, shaping life through an unceasing act of balance and restoration.

When I began to mirror this principle in my own life, even in the smallest ways, I understood the true nature of service. Whether it was speaking truth, helping a stranger, offering guidance without seeking recognition, or simply showing up with presence and authenticity, each act carried a significance beyond the moment.

Nothing done in truth is ever lost. Every expression of service ripples through eternity, expanding outward, touching lives in ways beyond our comprehension.

This is an invitation, an opportunity to step beyond the self and into something greater. To remove personal desire from service and allow the spirit to act without interference, without hesitation. We are not here to be worshipped, to be glorified for what we offer, or to attach our identity to the things we give.

We are here to work quietly, in the name of truth, in the name of harmony, in the name of Creation. And in that quiet work, we find something beyond fulfillment, we find purpose. The kind that does not waver, does not seek approval, but simply is.

CHAPTER 19:

Fear as a Teacher

For much of my life, fear ruled me, not in obvious ways, but in subtle, insidious forms that shaped my choices, limited my growth, and dictated the boundaries of my existence. It did not scream at me, nor did it appear as an overt force in my life. Instead, it whispered through hesitation, disguised itself as logic, and hid within the comfortable walls of avoidance.

I feared rejection, the possibility that my words, my truth, my very being might be dismissed or deemed inadequate. I feared judgment, the weight of others' opinions pressing against my desire to be understood. I feared failure, the unsettling idea that every attempt might end in disappointment, that mistakes would somehow define me.

And above all, I feared the unknown, what I could not predict, what I could not control, what waited beyond the edges of familiarity.

But through the Creation Energy Teachings, I came to a realization that fundamentally altered my relationship with fear. I learned that fear, too, plays an integral role in the path of evolution. It is not something to be rejected outright, nor is it an enemy to be battled into submission. Fear is a signal, a message that invites deeper understanding, revealing where we have yet to grow, where we hold resistance, where illusions have taken root in our minds.

When I stopped running from fear and instead faced it directly, I saw the fragile foundations upon which it was built. The vast majority of fear is not rooted in reality but in thought, images conjured by the mind, projections shaped by past experiences, distorted memories that hold us hostage to possibilities that may never come to pass. Fear thrives in uncertainty, feeding on hypothetical scenarios rather than the present truth.

In confronting my fear, I did not eradicate it completely. That was never the goal. Fear will always exist, it is part of life, part of the human condition. But I dissolved its power over me. I stopped allowing it to dictate my actions, to prevent me from stepping forward, to silence my voice.

Fear did not disappear, but it no longer controlled me. It became something I could walk with rather than be led by.

Through this process, I discovered a deeper meaning of courage. Courage is not the absence of fear. It is not an overwhelming force that crushes fear into nothingness. It is the commitment to truth in spite of fear, to move forward, to speak, to act even when uncertainty lingers.

It is the understanding that fear does not make us weak, avoidance does. And in facing fear head-on, we reclaim our power, our awareness, and our freedom.

This is my testament to the process of transmuting fear into clarity, one experience at a time. It is about learning to see fear for what it truly is, stripping away the illusions that surround it, and stepping forward with a mind no longer shackled by hesitation.

The more I understood fear, the less it had control over me. And now, I no longer walk behind it, I walk alongside it, knowing it is no longer my master, but a companion on the path of becoming.

CHAPTER 20:

Time and Timelessness

We measure life in hours, days, and years, believing that time is something we must chase, manage, or control. We build schedules, mark milestones, and define our worth by how efficiently we move through them. Yet, the spirit does not abide by these constraints. It exists beyond the ticking clock, beyond the structured timelines of human existence. The spirit lives in a realm of timeless awareness, where presence, not urgency, guides each moment.

For much of my life, I lived bound by time. I rushed through my days, chained to the dictates of schedules and calendars, constantly striving toward something just out of reach. Productivity defined my sense of purpose. I measured success by how much I accomplished, believing that to slow down was to fall behind.

I was always in pursuit, of more, of faster, of better. My close friends and some family members back in NY, especially my big sister Elsie, used to call me "the 100 miles per hour man". And yet, despite all my movement, I felt unfulfilled, disconnected from the deeper rhythm of existence.

But then, something shifted. I began to experience time differently, not as a relentless force to be conquered, but as a teacher, revealing the nature of presence. I came to see that Creation is not bound by our concept of linear time. It does not rush toward an endpoint or lament what has passed.

It exists in an eternal now, a space where all things unfold in perfect accordance with their own inherent timing. Nature does not force growth, it allows it. The stars do not hurry to shine, they emerge when their light is ready. The river does not demand its course, it follows where gravity and earth guide it.

With this realization, I learned to slow down. Not just in action, but in thought, in awareness, in the way I engaged with life itself. I listened, not to the demands of schedules, but to the quiet wisdom within. I let go of the frantic urgency that had once dictated my choices and instead began to trust that all things emerge in their rightful moment.

The need to force my path diminished. The pressure to always be ahead dissolved. I stepped into alignment with the natural flow of time.

And when I stopped resisting that flow, something profound occurred. I found presence, not as an idea, but as a lived reality. The past no longer bound me. The weight of old regrets, unfinished stories, and lingering memories ceased to hold authority over my present. The future no longer frightened me. I no longer felt the need to predict, control, or anxiously anticipate what had yet to arrive.

Instead, the now became my home, a space of clarity, where I could simply be, without expectation, without pressure.

This is an exploration of how to live in time without being enslaved by it, how to recognize that while we may move through time, we do not belong to it. When we align with Creation, we experience something beyond the limits of clocks and calendars. We step into timeless truth, finding eternity not as a distant destination but as the essence of our own awareness.

Eternity is not a place to reach. It is not something reserved for the distant future, nor an abstract concept beyond our grasp. It is our true nature, revealed in the depth of presence. It is here, now, waiting to be lived.

And when we surrender the urgency of time, we finally begin to experience life, not as a race, but as an unfolding, moment by moment, breath by breath.

CHAPTER 21:

Conscious Creation

We are not powerless wanderers, drifting aimlessly through existence, nor are we mere subjects to fate, bound by predetermined outcomes beyond our control. We are participants, active contributors to the unfolding reality of Creation itself. The circumstances of our lives are not written in stone, dictated solely by external forces. Rather, they are shaped by the energy we emit, the consciousness we cultivate, and the choices we make, whether knowingly or unconsciously.

Every thought, every feeling, every intention radiates outward, weaving itself into the fabric of possibility surrounding us. We are constantly creating, even when we do not realize it. Our minds generate frequencies that extend beyond mere words or actions, influencing the energetic field in ways imperceptible to the physical eye but undeniable in their impact. The teachings make this truth clear, consciousness precedes form. Reality does not exist independently of thought, it is guided by it, shaped by it, and altered by the currents we send forth.

This realization led me to examine the patterns of my own thinking, to question the energies I had unconsciously contributed to the world. I began to observe how my projections, whether rooted in fear, love, doubt, or clarity, were reflected back to me in the situations I encountered. I saw how negative thoughts attracted difficulty, how anger bred resistance, how peace cultivated more peace. Creation does not merely exist as a passive force, it listens, it mirrors, it amplifies. It takes what we send into it and returns it in kind.

With this understanding, I learned to be intentional, not only in my actions but in the frequency of my being. I became mindful of the energy

I carried, careful with the thoughts I allowed to settle in my consciousness, aware that every inner projection ultimately manifests externally. The more I aligned my mind with truth, the more my reality harmonized with peace. Resistance faded. Chaos settled. Clarity expanded.

This offers practical insight into the art of conscious co-creation, how to move beyond passive observation and step into the active role of shaping your own experience. Life is not something that simply happens to you. It is something you craft, something you bring into form through awareness, intention, and resonance.

Your life is your work of art. Each thought is a brushstroke, each feeling a shade of color, each decision a defining contour upon the canvas of existence. The question is, what are you painting?

When the inner world aligns with truth, the outer world follows. What lies within is inevitably reflected outward. To change the landscape of life, one must begin with the foundation of consciousness. This is not philosophy, it is the essence of Creation itself. And to grasp it, to live it, is to step fully into the role of a true creator. Not dictated by fate, but empowered by awareness. Not governed by limitation, but expanded by choice.

CHAPTER 22:

The Path of Peace

Peace is not the absence of struggle, nor is it a fragile state dependent on external conditions being perfectly aligned. It is not found in temporary stillness, nor does it require the elimination of conflict. True peace is not a passive retreat from chaos, it is the active presence of inner harmony, a steadiness that remains unshaken, regardless of what unfolds around it.

For years, I searched for peace outside myself. I believed it could be found in quieter circumstances, in favorable conditions, in a life free from hardship or disruption. I imagined that if only I could control my surroundings, structure my days perfectly, or eliminate sources of stress, I would finally feel at ease. But peace was always elusive because I was searching in the wrong place.

No matter how much I adjusted my environment, my mind remained restless. The world continued to move, bringing challenges, changes, and uncertainties that disrupted my carefully built illusion of tranquility.

Through the teachings of Creation, I came to understand a deeper truth, peace is not something we chase, it is something we cultivate within. It does not come from controlling life but from understanding it, accepting it, and transforming our relationship with it. I learned that true peace begins with self-peace, an internal reconciliation that allows us to forgive ourselves, love ourselves, and align with what is real rather than what we wish to be different.

As I embraced this internal work, something remarkable happened, peace expanded outward. It began to ripple into my relationships, softening old tensions and strengthening connections. It influenced my work, allowing me to approach challenges without resistance. It shaped my words, leading me to communicate with more kindness, more clarity, more presence.

I saw how peace is not just a personal state but an energy we extend into the world, a vibration that alters the spaces we enter, reshaping the very atmosphere around us.

True peace does not avoid discomfort. It does not demand that we escape difficult situations or suppress emotions that need to be understood. Instead, it meets every challenge with clarity and compassion, allowing us to engage with life without resistance, without fear. It is not passive, it is deeply active, requiring awareness, patience, and an unwavering commitment to truth.

Peace is not simply an idea, it is a frequency, an invisible force that transforms everything it touches. When cultivated with intention, it becomes something more than an internal experience, it becomes a presence that radiates outward, influencing the world in subtle yet profound ways.

This is both a reflection and a roadmap for cultivating unshakable peace. It is about stepping beyond theoretical discussions and stepping into lived experience, about embodying peace in every interaction, every thought, every action.

Because the world needs more than peace talks, it needs peace walks. It needs individuals who do not merely speak of balance and harmony but live it, breathe it, carry it into every space they enter.

Walk in peace, and you become a living teaching, not through words alone, but through the quiet, unwavering presence of a soul that has learned what peace truly is. It is not found in control, nor in isolation, nor in external perfection. It is found in alignment, with truth, with Creation, with the steady rhythm of existence itself. And when you embody it, the world cannot help but feel its presence.

CHAPTER 23:

Freedom Through Responsibility

F reedom and responsibility are not opposing forces, nor do they exist in contradiction. They are inseparable twins, interwoven, complementing each other in a way that many fail to recognize. True freedom is not the absence of responsibility but rather its fulfillment.

The deeper I stepped into my responsibility, for my thoughts, my choices, and my evolution, the freer I became. Liberation did not come from escaping obligation or rejecting accountability, it came from fully embracing the reality that I alone shape my experience.

Responsibility granted me sovereignty over my own life. No more blame. No more waiting for rescue. I stopped looking to external figures, governments, gurus, institutions, or gods, to dictate my path, to provide answers I was perfectly capable of discovering within myself.

I realized that outsourcing my power was the greatest act of self-denial. Every time I placed my fate in another's hands, I abandoned the authority I already possessed. But when I reclaimed responsibility, I reclaimed my strength.

The teachings are clear, only the one who lives by truth can be truly free. Truth does not bind, it clarifies. It dissolves illusions, removes dependency, and reveals the path to genuine autonomy.

I came to see that responsibility is not a weight, nor is it something to be avoided, it is the gateway to maturity, dignity, and the rarest form of self-trust. Without responsibility, freedom remains an illusion, a mere concept rather than a lived reality.

Many mistake responsibility for restriction. They view it as limitation, as something that confines rather than expands. But the opposite is true. Responsibility is alignment, the conscious choice to move with life rather than resist it. And in that alignment, there is nothing but freedom.

This is an invitation to stand in your power, not through dominance, not through control, but through deliberate choice. To recognize that freedom is not given, it is realized. It is not bestowed upon you, it is cultivated within you.

You are not meant to be ruled by external forces, nor dictated by the expectations of others. You are meant to be sovereign, to govern your own mind, shape your own life, and walk your own path with clarity and conviction.

CHAPTER 24:

The Great Return

All of life is a return, a spiraling, evolving journey back to the Source, gathering wisdom, refining awareness, and deepening our understanding with each experience. We do not move in straight lines, nor do we follow a predetermined road with a singular destination. We cycle, we expand, we contract, always reaching forward while remembering where we have come from.

I no longer fear where I am going because I have come to realize that I am not moving toward something unknown, I am returning to something deeply familiar. I carry the echoes of past understandings, the remnants of experiences that have shaped me across lifetimes, the silent call of truth that has always existed within.

The road does not lead away from myself, it leads me back, again and again, in layers, in cycles, in endless evolution.

The goal is not to escape the world, nor to transcend it as if it were something to be discarded. It is to live fully within it, consciously, lovingly, truthfully. To engage with it, to embrace its lessons, to meet its challenges with awareness and patience.

The world is not an obstacle, it is a teacher. And the deepest wisdom does not come from withdrawing but from participating, with open eyes, steady hands, and a spirit willing to learn.

I have walked many roads, questioned many truths, and stripped away illusions again and again. Each time I thought I had arrived at understanding, I found myself in silence. In that quiet space where all distractions fade, where all external definitions dissolve, I met myself, not the identity shaped by time and experience, but the essence that has always been.

And I know now that the journey is not linear, it is cyclical, infinite, eternal. We do not simply move forward, we spiral, returning to deeper versions of ourselves, seeing familiar truths from new vantage points, recognizing what has always been in ways we could not before.

We return, to ourselves, to Creation, to love. Not as we were, but as we are becoming. Not repeating, but expanding. Not retracing steps, but deepening into the truth we have touched before but are now ready to fully embrace.

This does not mark an ending, but rather an opening, an invitation to keep walking, keep growing, keep remembering. The journey does not conclude here, nor does it ever truly conclude. There is no final book, no ultimate arrival point. There is only the next experience, the next lesson, the next return.

So may your steps be steady, your heart open, and your mind clear. And when you arrive, wherever you are, know that the path continues. That I will meet you there, in the unfolding, in the remembering, in the great return, again and again.

CHAPTER 25:

Harmony With All Life

We cannot truly evolve, spiritually, emotionally, or collectively, while continuing to harm the life that surrounds us. True growth is not just upward but outward, encompassing all the beings with whom we share this world.

There is a deeper law at work in the universe, one of harmony, balance, and interdependence. This law is not enforced through control, but through resonance. All of Creation, from the stars above to the soil beneath our feet, abides by it.

Over time, I began to perceive something profound, every living being I once considered "other," every animal, tree, river, bird, and insect, is not separate from me, but rather another unique expression of Creation itself.

Each form of life is a mirror, a reflection of the same sacred force that animates me. There is no "them" in nature. There is only "us," manifesting in infinite ways.

Disharmony begins the moment we forget this. When we see ourselves as separate, superior, or entitled to take without giving, we lose our place in the sacred web. We create imbalance, not only in the world around us, but within ourselves.

When I began to treat the Earth as holy ground, and each living being as family, each with its own wisdom, purpose, and place, something within me shifted. My energy softened. I felt more grounded, more complete. It was as though I had returned to a forgotten truth I had always known.

The teachings revealed to me that harmony is not simply the absence of conflict, it is the presence of right relationship. It is reciprocity, mutual care, and deep listening.

This understanding changed the way I lived. I began to move more mindfully, to eat with reverence, to speak and act with greater care. These changes did not come from guilt or fear, but from awareness.

Harmony is not a concept to admire from afar. It is the natural rhythm of life itself. When we align with it, life ceases to be a struggle and begins to feel like music.

CHAPTER 26:

The End of Worship.

One of the most liberating and transformative moments on this path came when I stopped worshipping and began honoring. It was as if a veil lifted, and I could finally see with clarity the subtle difference between these two ways of relating to the sacred. Worship, as I had come to know it, placed the divine on a pedestal far above me, casting me in the role of the small, the unworthy, the dependent. It created a sense of distance, of separation, of needing to earn love or favor from something beyond myself.

Honor, on the other hand, is intimate. It is rooted in reverence, mutual recognition, and deep love. To honor something is to see its essence clearly and to treat it with respect, not because we fear it, but because we understand its value and its place in the great web of life. Honor affirms connection. It restores balance. It awakens a sense of equality between the spark of spirit within me and the larger forces that surround me.

I came to understand that Creation does not ask to be worshipped in fear or blind obedience. It does not seek our songs of praise if they are not lived in alignment. What it asks, what it yearns for, is to be seen, known, and respected. The Earth does not demand temples, it asks for care. The wind does not require prayers, it invites presence. The divine is not somewhere else, waiting to be appeased, it is here, in everything, waiting to be honored through how we live.

This realization shook the foundations of what I once believed. I saw how worship had been used, often unconsciously, to strip us of our inner power. By placing gods, idols, or rigid doctrines above ourselves, we often abdicate our responsibility. We wait to be saved. We look for answers outside. We diminish the light within us and call it humility.

But the spirit within me was not created to grovel or kneel in shame. It was born to grow, to evolve, to awaken into its full truth. The divine spark is not outside of us, it is within, pulsing in every breath, guiding us not toward submission, but toward self-realization.

The teachings that truly resonated with me did not demand worship. They invited understanding. The wise ones, the sages, the sacred teachers I encountered, whether through books, through nature, or through inner experience or through meeting the Herald himself and spending time with him, they all pointed beyond themselves. They did not say, "Follow me,

And so, I stopped worshipping and started walking in honor. Honor for the Earth, which feeds and holds me. Honor for truth, which challenges and liberates me. Honor for all life, which reflects the many faces of the sacred. I no longer feel the need to kneel in fear or obedience. Instead, I bow in gratitude, in kinship, in recognition.

This is about reclaiming your inner sovereignty, the power to see, to know, to live in alignment with what is real. It is about ending the cycles of dependency and illusion that keep us small, and stepping into the maturity of spiritual responsibility.

Stop worshipping what you were told to fear. Start honoring what you truly know to be sacred. Live the truth that burns quietly, steadily, within your own soul.

CHAPTER 27:

The Purpose of Suffering.

There was a time when I saw suffering as punishment, something unfair, something to escape, something that signaled I had done something wrong or was being tested by a harsh universe. I viewed pain as the enemy, a sign that life had turned against me. My instinct was to avoid it, suppress it, or resent it, doing everything I could to stay comfortable and in control.

But over time, as I walked this path and listened more deeply to the rhythms of Creation, I was shown a different way of seeing. Suffering, I came to understand, is not a curse but a call. It is not retribution, but revelation. It carries within it the seeds of awakening, if we are willing to listen.

Creation began to show me that suffering can serve a sacred purpose. It can act as a mirror, reflecting the places where I am out of balance, out of alignment with truth. Pain, when met with awareness, becomes a signal, a messenger that arrives not to torment us, but to guide us back to ourselves. It is often the soul's way of whispering, "There is something here you must see. Something you must change."

I realized that much of my suffering had come not from the pain itself, but from my resistance to it. When I pushed it away, when I buried it beneath distractions or denial, it only grew heavier. But when I turned toward it with openness and asked, "What is this here to teach me?", everything shifted. Suffering became a doorway, not a dead end.

Rather than drowning in self-pity or blame, I began to approach my pain with curiosity and reverence. I started to see it as a teacher, often a fierce one, but always purposeful. Each wound became an invitation to greater clarity, to deeper strength, to more expansive compassion. My suffering, when embraced and understood, became alchemical. It transformed me from within.

This is not to romanticize pain or suggest that all suffering is necessary. There is much in the world that is cruel, unjust, and should be healed. We must work to end unnecessary suffering wherever we find it, in ourselves, in others, and in the systems we live within. But even as we do, we must not discard the wisdom suffering can offer. The pain we move through with consciousness can leave behind medicine, insight, humility, resilience, empathy.

This invites us to reframe our relationship with suffering. Instead of viewing it as failure or misfortune, we can begin to see it as a spiritual companion, a sacred teacher that, when honored, can help us shed illusions and come into deeper truth. Suffering is not the destination, it is the passage.

The goal is never to glorify suffering, but to grow through and beyond it. To let it refine us, not define us. To use its fire not to burn us down, but to forge us into something more whole, more awake, more loving.

In the light of truth, even sorrow holds beauty. Even grief has grace. And when we stop running from pain and begin to meet it with presence, we find that within the heart of suffering, there is something holy, something waiting to heal us, if we are willing to receive its wisdom.

CHAPTER 28:

The Sacredness of Work.

In the spiritual life, nothing is ordinary or insignificant, not even work. There was a time when I believed spiritual practice existed separately from the daily responsibilities of life, as though the sacred could be compartmentalized and kept apart from worldly tasks. But the teachings unveiled a profound truth, everything is spiritual. Every action, every moment, and every endeavor holds the potential to be an expression of the divine.

Work, then, is not merely an obligation or a means to an end. It is a sacred field where we cultivate awareness, embody love, and serve with devotion. No matter what the task, whether writing, sweeping, building, teaching, or even tending to the simplest of chores, it carries significance. It reflects our inner state, our consciousness, and our ability to act in harmony with creation.

When we approach our work with presence and care, it becomes more than labor, it transforms into an offering, a direct communion with the sacred.

I used to work simply to survive, to earn, or to impress. But when I embraced a higher understanding, everything shifted. My motivation was no longer rooted in external validation or mere necessity. Instead, I worked to express my inner alignment, to bring forth the essence of my spirit in every act. In doing so, I found that my work stopped feeling like a burden and instead became a source of fulfillment.

The teachings speak of "creation-conforming" work, labor that uplifts, serves, and does no harm to oneself or others. When work is approached with such intentionality, it nourishes both the body and the soul, deepening one's connection to life itself.

Bringing spirit into my work was a revelation. It infused my actions with a sense of purpose, transforming the ordinary into the extraordinary. As a house cleaner, I can attest to this truth. I no longer viewed effort as something to endure but as a pathway to growth, joy, and evolution.

This is a tribute to the sacred nature of human activity and the dignity of conscious effort. For when work is rightly understood, it ceases to be a mundane duty and becomes a radiant expression of one's spiritual journey.

CHAPTER 29:

Facing Death, Living Fully.

Nothing awakens the soul quite like confronting the truth of mortality. It is the great equalizer, the force that humbles even the mightiest among us and reminds us that every moment is fleeting, every heartbeat precious. To understand death is to understand life itself, for they are intertwined, two sides of the same eternal rhythm.

I no longer fear death, because I have come to see it not as a finality, but as a transition, one that unfolds with wisdom and purpose. The body may perish, but the spirit does not die. It moves forward, it gathers knowledge, it evolves beyond the limitations of physical existence.

With this understanding, I began to live in a radically different way. I no longer measured my days in anxieties and expectations, but in presence and depth. Regrets faded, replaced by a sharper clarity of purpose. The preciousness of time became my guide, leading me to decisions rooted in authenticity rather than obligation.

Death, rather than an ominous specter, became my advisor. It whispered profound truths, "Do not delay truth. Do not postpone love. Do not waste time chasing illusions." These words reshaped my world.

I let go of the burdens that weighed me down, superficial worries, artificial attachments, the need to prove myself in ways that no longer mattered. Instead, I deepened my commitments to the things that truly nourished my soul. I simplified my life, stripping away excess until only the essential remained: love, purpose, integrity, presence.

The teachings remind us that to fear death is, in truth, to fear life itself. Both are governed by the same fundamental law of impermanence. To resist one is to resist the other. But when we embrace the transient nature of existence, we unlock a profound liberation. In relinquishing the illusion of permanence, we step into the fullness of every moment, unafraid and unburdened.

This invites a new relationship with impermanence, one that is not rooted in avoidance, but in wisdom, courage, and reverence. It urges us to see life not as a series of ticking hours leading toward an inevitable end, but as a sacred journey where every breath carries meaning.

To live well is to prepare for death, not through fear or hesitation, but by choosing wholeness now. In accepting mortality, we step into our truest existence. We cease merely surviving and, finally, become fully alive.

CHAPTER 30:

Simplicity is Strength.

In a world that constantly pushes us toward more, more possessions, more responsibilities, more distractions, simplicity stands as a radical, almost rebellious choice. It is not just about clearing space or reducing clutter. It is a deeply intentional act, a conscious decision to strip away what does not serve, so that what remains can shine with clarity and purpose.

I discovered that as I simplified, I became clearer, not just in my surroundings, but in my thoughts, in my commitments, and in my direction. Complexity, I realized, often masks uncertainty, fear, and even self-doubt. It provides an illusion of progress, of movement, but often leaves us tangled in a web of confusion.

Simplicity, on the other hand, reveals truth. It clears the fog, allowing us to see the essence of things as they truly are.

The teachings urge us toward clarity, not clutter, to embrace essence over excess. I started letting go of everything that weighed me down, the noise of unnecessary worries, the distractions pulling my attention in countless directions, the possessions that I had accumulated but no longer truly needed, and even the old beliefs that no longer aligned with the person I was becoming.

With each release, I felt lighter. I found that what remained was profound, peace that was undisturbed, presence that was fully engaged, and power that came not from external validation but from inner certainty.

Simplicity does not mean deprivation. It is not about lacking, but about refining. It is the art of knowing what truly matters and having the wisdom to prioritize it above all else. It is elegance, an unburdened existence where every choice is made with thoughtfulness, every action carries intention, and nothing is wasted on the unnecessary.

This delves into the heart of simplicity, not just as a lifestyle, but as a philosophy, a way of approaching existence with mindfulness and purpose. It is an invitation to simplify not just the external aspects of life, but the self, to untangle the complexities of identity, to shed the layers that obscure authenticity, and to embrace the quiet, powerful truth of being.

In simplicity, the voice of the spirit becomes louder. The distractions fade, and what remains is the raw, unfiltered essence of life itself. When we choose less, we do not lose, we gain. We discover more than we ever thought possible.

CHAPTER 31:

The Joy of Being Alone.

We often recoil at the thought of solitude, mistaking it for the cold ache of loneliness. But solitude is not isolation, nor is it deprivation, it is a sacred sanctuary, a realm where the spirit speaks with unparalleled clarity, where distractions fall away, and truth emerges. It is in stillness, in silence, in the vast openness of aloneness that we begin to truly meet ourselves, beyond the masks we wear, beyond the expectations imposed upon us, beyond the fleeting identities that we cling to.

For so long, I feared emptiness. I filled every gap with noise, with movement, with the company of others, never pausing long enough to hear what lay beneath. But when I finally stopped running, when I surrendered to the quiet, I realized that emptiness was not the void I had imagined. It was spaciousness, possibility, a canvas for transformation. I began listening to it, and in return, it whispered lessons I had long ignored.

The teachings affirm that solitude is not only valuable, it is necessary for evolution. Time alone is not a punishment, but a gift, a space where we refine our awareness, cultivate inner strength, and nurture our intuition. It is within solitude that we come to enjoy our own presence, not as a role we play, nor as a constructed identity, but as pure consciousness, vast and limitless.

With this realization, I became less needy, less dependent on external validation or the fleeting comfort of distractions. I no longer feared being alone, because I understood that solitude had never abandoned me, it had always been waiting, patiently, for my return. In its embrace, I found stability. I deepened my intuition. I rooted myself more firmly in my own existence.

This is a call to reclaim aloneness, not as exile, not as something to endure, but as a homecoming. It is an invitation to shed the illusion that our worth is measured by company or constant engagement. To be alone is not to be lost, it is to be present with the one person who has walked every step of our journey, ourselves.

In solitude, the illusions dissolve, and the essence shines. The noise fades, revealing the quiet pulse of truth that has always been there, beneath the surface. So be still. Be alone. Not because you must, but because there is beauty in that space. There is wisdom. There is wholeness. And in it, you finally meet yourself.

CHAPTER 32:

Forgiveness as Liberation.

Forgiveness is not forgetting. It is the conscious act of unshackling yourself from the weight of past wounds, freeing your spirit from the prison of resentment. It does not erase what has happened, nor does it deny the impact of pain. Instead, it is a profound choice, a refusal to let suffering dictate the course of one's life.

For a long time, I carried wounds that blurred my vision and drained my energy. They shaped my thoughts, hardened my heart, and burdened my steps. The grievances of yesterday clung to me, weaving themselves into my present, distorting my view of the world. I told myself that holding onto anger was strength, that remembering every betrayal was a form of self-protection. But in truth, it was a weight I could not bear, a poison slowly eroding my peace.

When I forgave, I did not dismiss the harm done. I did not justify or forget the injustices. Instead, I chose to sever the invisible chains that had bound me to pain for so long. I learned that forgiveness is not about condoning hurtful actions, it is about refusing to let them continue harming me. It is not a gift to those who inflicted harm, but an act of liberation for myself. In releasing anger, I reclaimed my power. In surrendering bitterness, I restored my inner clarity.

The teachings revealed that forgiveness does not always require reconciliation. Some wounds do not mend in reunion, some people do not belong in your journey forward. Yet, even in the absence of closure from others, I discovered that I could grant myself the resolution I needed. I could choose peace, even if the past remained unchanged. I could let go without waiting for an apology that might never come.

And then came a deeper realization, one that transformed me in ways I never expected. I understood that true forgiveness could not only be extended outward, it also had to turn inward. I carried guilt, regrets, mistakes I could not outrun. I had punished myself for my own missteps, held myself hostage to the past in ways I had never held others. But just as resentment toward others is spiritual poison, so too is self-condemnation. I had to forgive myself, to grant my own being the same grace I had learned to offer others.

With each act of release, I felt lighter, clearer, freer. I was no longer tethered to the burdens of yesterday. I no longer lived in the shadows of past pain. Forgiveness became my pathway to healing, not through denial but through wisdom, the wisdom to see that clinging to sorrow does not change what has been, but releasing it can transform what is yet to come.

This explores both the mechanics and the mysticism of true forgiveness. It is not about deciding who deserves absolution, it is about choosing to reclaim your own peace. It is about understanding that forgiveness is not weakness, it is courage in its purest form. It is strength woven with wisdom, the boldness to break free from the suffering that no longer serves your spirit.

To forgive is not to surrender, it is to rise. It is to choose wholeness over wounds, freedom over bondage, and life over lingering pain. It is wisdom, illuminated in action.

CHAPTER 33:

The Spiral of Self-Mastery.

Self-mastery is not the pursuit of flawless perfection, it is the ongoing, lifelong process of refinement. It is the patient, deliberate work of shaping oneself, not through grand gestures or sudden epiphanies, but through quiet discipline, steady growth, and the deepening of awareness.

I once thought that transformation came through breakthroughs, those rare, dramatic moments of insight where everything shifts at once. But with time, I realized that mastery is not about sudden leaps forward, it is about constancy. It is about showing up, day after day, with presence and intention. It is about the small, consistent acts of learning, adjusting, and aligning, again and again.

Mastery is not a spectacle, it does not announce itself with fanfare. Instead, it resides in the stillness of observation, in the practice of awareness, in the humility of self-examination. It is the willingness to ask, What do I need to refine? Where am I out of balance? How can I act with greater integrity? Each day, I take note. Each day, I make adjustments, not to force myself into an unattainable ideal, but to allow my most truthful self to emerge.

The teachings describe life as a spiral, a path we walk again and again, revisiting familiar lessons, encountering old patterns, but always at a higher level. Growth is not linear, nor is it a straight ascent. It is a rhythm, a cycle, an unfolding. The same challenges may arise, but each time, we meet them with deeper wisdom, with a steadier mind, with a heart that has learned patience. Mastery does not mean never faltering, it means recognizing the pattern, understanding the lesson, and moving forward with greater clarity.

There are no shortcuts on this path. No sudden way to bypass the necessary work of presence, practice, and patience. Mastery is earned through experience, through persistence, through the willingness to keep refining, even when the progress is slow. It is not about control, it is about surrendering to the truth of what is, and working with it rather than against it.

I no longer seek to dominate the self, to bend it into submission. Instead, I seek to understand it, to evolve it with care. Mastery is not about rigid discipline, it is about fluid wisdom. It is knowing when to hold steady and when to let go. It is trusting in the process, even when it feels uncertain.

True mastery is humility. It is the recognition that we are always learning, always growing, always arriving at new depths of understanding. It is not about becoming superior, it is about serving truth with integrity, about aligning action with essence.

This is an invitation to embrace your own spiral path, not with frustration, but with reverence. Not with the demand for perfection, but with the quiet determination to keep walking, keep refining, keep becoming. You are not meant to be flawless. You are meant to be whole. And with each step, with each lesson, with each moment of awareness, you come closer to that wholeness. Not suddenly. Not dramatically. But steadily. Faithfully. With love and resolve.

CHAPTER 34:

Becoming the Teaching.

B ooks, teachers, and words hold immense value. They shape perspectives, ignite transformation, and illuminate paths. But they are not the destination. They are guideposts, tools, stepping stones, but never the goal itself. The true purpose of learning, of absorbing wisdom, is not to merely understand it intellectually, but to embody it fully. To become a living expression of the truth, rather than simply speaking about it.

I once thought that wisdom was found in eloquence, that understanding came from accumulating knowledge and sharing it convincingly. But with time, I learned that wisdom is not measured by how many words one speaks, nor by how many teachings one can quote. True wisdom is lived, it is expressed through action, through presence, through quiet integrity. When you embody a teaching, you do not need to persuade or prove yourself. Your very existence becomes a testament to what you know in your soul.

As I deepened my journey, I began to see my life not just as a collection of experiences, but as a message in itself. Not perfect, not without struggle, but faithful, faithful to the lessons I had learned, to the truth I sought, to the intentions I cultivated. Every choice, every interaction, every moment became a reflection of my inner alignment, a mirror of what I valued most.

The teachings remind us that wisdom is not something external to chase, it is something internal to realize. We are simultaneously the vessel, the student, and the lesson. We hold truth within us, and it is only when we cease searching for it outside ourselves that we begin to truly understand.

This is not an ending. It does not signal completion, because there is no final destination in this path. Instead, it is a commission, an invitation to stop carrying words as mere concepts and start living them as tangible reality. It urges us to release the need to recite wisdom and instead become it, to let truth manifest in our being, to let understanding shine through our presence, to let our lives serve as a quiet but undeniable testament to what we know to be real.

So let these words dissolve. Let them drift away like leaves in the wind, until only the essence remains. And in that stillness, let your life speak. Let your existence radiate the truth you have touched, the wisdom you have cultivated, the understanding that cannot be confined to language.

Become the teaching. Not as something outside yourself, but as the truest form of yourself. Let truth walk through you, no longer as an idea to grasp, but as a force to embody. Let it shape your actions, refine your presence, and illuminate the path, not only for yourself but for all who encounter you.

CHAPTER 35:

The Power of Neutrality.

Neutrality is often misunderstood as indifference, a dull, detached stance where one refuses to engage. But in reality, neutrality is far from passive. It is mastery over emotional reaction, the ability to hold oneself steady in the midst of extremes. It is the skill of seeing clearly, beyond personal bias, beyond fear, beyond the pull of conditioned responses. It is the art of maintaining equilibrium, not because one does not care, but because clarity is more valuable than impulsivity.

For much of my life, I was driven by extremes. I saw the world in sharp contrasts, love or hate, hope or despair, certainty or doubt. I assumed passion meant intensity, that conviction required emotional weight. Yet, the teachings unveiled a different truth, balance does not reside in polarity. It resides in the center, where wisdom is unshaken, where perception is undistorted, where choices are made not from reaction, but from deep discernment.

Neutrality granted me the ability to pause, to step back from the urgency of feeling and observe with intention. It allowed me to witness the full scope of situations without attachment to immediate judgments. And in that pause, a new kind of power emerged, the ability to choose wisely, to act with precision rather than impulse.

I came to understand that neutrality is not a lack of engagement, it is a refinement of engagement. It is choosing what deserves energy and what does not. It is knowing when to speak and when to remain silent.

It is potent, not passive. A calm mind is a sharp sword, cutting through illusion, slicing away excess emotion that clouds judgment. Neutrality is not avoidance, it is the highest form of presence. It requires effort, discipline, and conscious awareness. It demands that one remains steady while the storm rages, anchored while the world sways in turbulence.

Through neutrality, I learned to respond rather than react. To pause before forming conclusions. To listen longer, observe deeper, and understand before judging. This shift made me less shaken by chaos, less vulnerable to external turmoil, less entangled in the emotional storms of others. It grounded me in a peace that was not fragile, not conditional, but rooted in something immovable.

This is an offering, a reminder that neutrality is the birthplace of wisdom. It is the space where truth has the room to rise unobstructed, where clarity emerges without distortion, where actions stem from understanding rather than impulse.

In the quiet of neutrality, truth does not have to fight to be heard. It simply rises, unchallenged, unwavering, illuminating everything in its path. The invitation here is not to disengage, but to master the art of standing in stillness while the world moves around you. To embrace neutrality as a tool, as a guide, as a foundation from which true wisdom can emerge.

CHAPTER 36:

Inner Technology.

T he world relentlessly pursues external technology, machines, gadgets, artificial intelligence, always seeking greater efficiency, more innovation, faster progress. Yet, in this race toward outer advancement, we often overlook the most powerful and sophisticated tool ever created, human consciousness. Before there were algorithms, circuits, or digital networks, there was the mind, the original processor, the eternal source of creativity, intelligence, and transformation.

Through my journey, I discovered that my thoughts, emotions, and spirit were not merely abstract experiences but a form of living technology, an intricate system capable of shaping reality itself. The teachings revealed profound truths, that thoughts influence matter, that intention carries energy, that consciousness, when harnessed with clarity, has the power to direct the course of existence.

I realized that just as a computer requires precise coding and calibration, my own inner world required refinement, focus, and mastery.

So I began treating my inner life with discipline, not as something chaotic and unpredictable, but as something to be understood, optimized, and aligned. Meditation became my control panel, a way to adjust settings, clear disturbances, and fine-tune perception. Silence became my reset, the place where I cleared outdated programs, removed mental clutter, and restored balance.

Every breath, every moment of mindfulness, became an act of conscious programming, rewriting patterns of thought, shifting emotional responses, and refining my inner frequency.

I saw the human being not as a mere biological entity, but as a multidimensional instrument of evolution. We are equipped with extraordinary capabilities, knowing, healing, creating, transforming, yet most of us never learn to operate ourselves with intention. We move unconsciously, driven by reactive forces, unaware of the immense potential encoded within us.

But when we awaken to our inner technology, when we learn to work with it rather than against it, we unlock abilities that go far beyond the physical realm.

This explores the design and limitless potential of the inner human system, our built-in intelligence, our ability to perceive beyond logic, our innate capacity to shape reality with thought and energy. We are not crude beings of chance, nor are we bound by limitations imposed by external forces. We are engineered for expansion, designed for mastery, equipped with everything we need to evolve beyond what we once believed possible.

Awaken your inner technology. Learn the language of your own mind, the rhythm of your own spirit, the mechanics of your own power. When you master the self, external tools become secondary. True advancement begins from within.

CHAPTER 37:

The Spirit Never Sleeps.

Even when the body finds stillness, even when the mind drifts into slumber, the spirit remains active, ceaselessly moving, seeking, expanding. It does not obey the limitations of time or space. It does not fatigue, does not falter, does not wait for permission to evolve. It is the pulse beneath existence, the guiding force behind awareness, the unseen current shaping every moment.

I discovered that the whispers of the spirit manifest in many ways, through dreams that speak in symbols, through intuition that bypasses logic, through synchronicities that reveal unseen patterns. These are not coincidences, they are messages. The teachings tell us that spirit is eternal, tireless, and ever-expanding. Unlike the personality, which shifts with circumstances, the spirit holds a singular devotion, to grow, to awaken, to move beyond limitation.

I learned that the spirit does not shout. It does not demand. It does not force its way into awareness. It nudges. It signals. It calls softly. And it waits. It waits for us to listen.

For so long, I dismissed these signs as insignificant, as random occurrences or figments of imagination. But when I began listening more deeply, when I leaned into what moved me, what stirred me, what pulled my attention without explanation, I realized that my life was not a series of disconnected events. It was orchestrated, woven together by something unseen but ever-present.

The spirit does not communicate in language, nor does it rely on structured thought. It speaks in knowing, in felt truths that arise without analysis, in sensations that bypass intellect and land directly in the heart. Its voice is recognized not by sound but by resonance, when something feels undeniably right, even if the mind has no proof.

This is an invitation, a call to deepen your relationship with the spirit within you, to understand that it is not an observer of your life but the navigator steering its course. It is not merely present, it is active, shaping, guiding, leading. If you are willing to hear, if you are willing to trust, the spirit will unfold its wisdom before you.

And in that trust, a transformation occurs. Life ceases to feel chaotic and begins to feel intentional. You stop chasing logic and start following knowing. You move not from fear, but from alignment. You realize that truth does not need external validation, it only requires recognition.

So trust the spirit. It never sleeps, never hesitates, never deceives. It is the one force that has never abandoned you, never misled you, never failed you. Let it guide you. Let it remind you who you truly are. Let it move, unrestrained, unquestioned, unhindered, toward the depths of your highest becoming.

CHAPTER 38:

True Peace is Earned.

Peace is not something handed to us, nor is it a fleeting gift bestowed by circumstance. It is something cultivated, through alignment, through effort, through a deep and enduring maturity. It does not arrive by chance, nor does it linger without intention. It is built, slowly, steadily, with each choice we make, with each layer of illusion we remove, with each truth we embrace.

I once thought peace was a prize, a reward for enduring hardship or proving myself worthy. I thought it would come when life settled, when difficulties faded, when everything finally aligned in my favor. But through the teachings, I came to understand that peace is not an external event, it is an internal creation. It is not something we wait for, but something we cultivate, something we construct through our own inner work.

I learned that true peace cannot coexist with unresolved inner conflict. If my mind was tangled in contradictions, if my heart was burdened by fear, if my spirit was clouded by illusions, then no amount of external calm could grant me peace. I had to go inward. I had to face myself completely.

I had to work through the distortions that kept me fragmented, the unexamined thoughts that pulled me in opposite directions, the fears that whispered doubt into my quietest moments.

It was not easy. There were painful truths I had to acknowledge, wounds I had to heal, attachments I had to release. But with every layer cleared, with every illusion dismantled, I felt something shift. Peace was no longer an abstract hope, it became tangible. It revealed itself not as the absence of struggle, but as the presence of truth. And the more I stood in that truth, the more unshakable my peace became.

Real peace does not waver with circumstances. It does not crumble under pressure or disappear when life grows chaotic. It is a state of being, a foundation that remains intact regardless of the shifting tides of experience. It is rooted in something deeper than comfort, deeper than certainty, deeper than the fleeting quiet of an undisturbed day.

It is anchored in clarity, in the unwavering knowing of who you are, what you stand for, and what truly matters.

This is not about passive serenity. It is not about waiting for peace to arrive. It is a manual for the inner work required to construct true peace, to make it a lasting force within you, independent of conditions. Because peace is not a dream, nor is it a distant ideal. It is a discipline. It is the practiced commitment to truth, to balance, to self-mastery.

Peace is possible, not for those who wish for it, not for those who seek to escape discomfort, but for those willing to walk the path of truth. Those willing to clear the inner clutter, to resolve what needs resolution, to refine themselves into vessels of stillness amidst movement, of clarity amidst chaos.

If you choose that path, peace will not be a fleeting moment, it will be the foundation upon which your entire existence rests.

CHAPTER 39:

Time is a Creation Tool.

I once feared time. I saw it as a relentless force, pressing forward without mercy, shrinking my possibilities, stealing my days. It felt like a constant countdown, a looming presence reminding me that everything, every joy, every opportunity, every dream, had an expiration date. I viewed time as limitation, as a slow march toward inevitable endings, as a reminder that nothing lasts forever.

But the teachings shifted my perception entirely. I learned that time is not an enemy, nor is it something to resist. Time is a tool of Creation, an intelligent force, shaping, guiding, refining. It does not steal, it reveals. It does not rush, it prepares.

I began to see how timing was not arbitrary but deeply intentional, aligning us with lessons, unfolding growth in ways we do not always understand until much later. What seemed like delays were, in truth, refinements. What felt like waiting was actually gestation, preparing me for what I was not yet ready to receive.

I stopped rushing. I stopped grasping at moments, trying to control their pace, trying to force outcomes before their rightful time. Instead, I began working with time rather than against it, flowing with its rhythm rather than struggling to dictate it.

This shift changed everything. Each moment ceased to feel like something fleeting, slipping through my grasp. Instead, each became a container of potential, holding within it exactly what was needed for that stage of my journey.

I let go of the impatient question, "When?", the anxious demand for timing to bend to my desires. In its place, a wiser question emerged: "What must I become?" Because time does not simply deliver, it responds. It aligns with readiness. It does not hold things back out of cruelty, it holds them back because they are not yet fully formed.

The spiral of time returns us again and again, not to repeat, but to refine, to allow us to meet familiar lessons with new wisdom, new depth, new strength.

This encourages a sacred patience, a willingness to be in full participation with the unfolding rather than fighting against it. It asks us to step away from the illusion that we are behind, that life is slipping through our fingers, that we must race to keep up.

Because the truth is, we are not losing time. We are arriving. Each stage, each lesson, each experience comes precisely when it should, not a moment too soon, not a moment too late.

Time is not a thief. It is a sculptor, carefully shaping us, chiseling away illusions, refining edges, preparing us for the next stage of expansion. And when we stop resisting, when we trust its rhythm, we cease to fear it.

Instead, we learn to stand in it fully, embracing each moment for exactly what it holds, no longer counting down, but opening up. No longer fearing the passage of time, but understanding it as the ultimate guide, leading us toward our highest becoming.

CHAPTER 40:

Nature is the Living Book.

Long before written language carved symbols onto parchment, truth was etched in the rhythms of the earth, the concentric rings of ancient trees, the ceaseless flow of rivers shaping the land, the silent choreography of birds tracing paths across the sky. Before humans codified knowledge into books, Nature had already composed its own sacred text, an unbroken dialogue spoken through movement, through balance, through the seamless interaction of all living things.

The teachings revealed to me that Creation does not whisper its wisdom in obscurity, it speaks through Nature with unfiltered clarity. Open, direct, unobstructed by the distortions of human interpretation. It is there, in the patient rise of the sun, in the slow unfolding of seasons, in the quiet intelligence of the ecosystem, that the truth is laid bare, waiting to be observed.

I began to listen. To pause in the presence of trees, to sit beneath the vast expanse of stars, to let water teach me its steady, unrelenting wisdom. I stopped looking at Nature as scenery and began seeing it as scripture.

Each encounter became a lesson, each bird a message, each cycle a mirror. The movements of the sky spoke to me of constancy. The stillness of the forest revealed the power of patience. The shifting tides demonstrated surrender, flow, adaptation.

Nature taught me not only presence, but precision. Not only patience, but purpose. It showed me that life does not thrive by force, by conquest, by unchecked control, but through rhythm, through balance, through symbiotic respect.

Every creature plays a role, every element contributes, every interaction serves the whole. When I truly understood this, I stopped seeing Earth as a resource to be consumed and started recognizing it as a classroom, an infinite source of wisdom beyond anything written by human hands.

This is an invitation, not to simply admire nature but to read it, to absorb its teachings, to recognize its ancient intelligence as guidance meant for us all. To step beyond the limitations of human knowledge and enter the vast domain of universal truth, where lessons unfold without words, without lectures, without formulas, only presence.

Return to the living book. Stand among trees and listen to the quiet hum beneath their bark. Watch the way water carves landscapes without resistance. Observe the cycles that govern all life, the endless renewal, the natural balance, the unseen forces that maintain harmony.

Nature speaks. Truth echoes. And it waits, not to be studied, but to be understood. Not to be used, but to be honored. If you listen, you will hear. If you watch, you will learn. If you trust, the wisdom will unfold in ways you never expected.

CHAPTER 41:

The Law of Becoming.

Nothing in Creation remains static. Everything, every particle, every being, every thought, is in continuous motion, expanding, contracting, shifting, growing. The universe does not cling to stagnation, it moves forward, always unfolding, always evolving. Change is not an exception, it is the very law upon which existence is built.

For a long time, I resisted this truth. I clung to familiarity, mistaking comfort for stability, mistaking stillness for security. I feared change, saw it as loss, as disruption, as something imposed rather than something intrinsic to life itself. But the teachings revealed what I had overlooked, change is not a force that works against us, it is the process through which we become.

I began to understand that transformation is not a departure from who we are but an arrival into a deeper version of ourselves. Even mistakes, even struggles, even the moments we wish we could undo, they all serve a purpose. Growth is woven into the design of life, it is not something we must force, but something we must trust. The caterpillar does not need permission to become a butterfly, it simply follows the law of its nature, dissolving what was to give way to what will be.

So I stopped resisting. I stopped grasping at old versions of myself, stopped fearing the dissolution of identities that had once defined me. I understood that those past versions were scaffolds, necessary structures that held me in place until I was ready to expand beyond them. Their disappearance was not a loss, it was an evolution.

Becoming is not always easy. It requires surrender, patience, and faith in the unseen. There are moments when growth feels like unraveling, when progress feels like destruction, when the transformation itself feels unbearable. But the teachings remind us, becoming is always sacred. It is the most natural process in the universe, the shedding, the renewal, the continuous movement toward expansion.

This is a celebration of transformation, an acknowledgment of the beauty and difficulty of evolution, and a roadmap through it. It is here to remind you that you are not failing, you are not falling apart, you are not stuck, you are unfolding. You are shifting into the next iteration of yourself, following the invisible rhythm of your own becoming.

You are not broken. You are in motion. Trust that motion. Allow it. Let it carve away what no longer serves, let it illuminate what has been waiting to emerge. Stop fearing change and start flowing with its wisdom.

Let the process work. Let the truth rise. And when you look back, you will see, every moment of transformation led you exactly where you needed to be.

CHAPTER 42:

Integrity as Alignment.

Integrity is not about appearances, nor is it about conforming to ideas of virtue imposed by others. It is not about being "good" in a way that pleases the outside world. It is about alignment, deep, unwavering congruence between the inner self and the outer expression. It is about living without contradiction, about ensuring that one's thoughts, words, and actions move in harmony rather than dissonance.

For much of my life, I performed virtue. I did what seemed honorable, what was praised, what fit the expectations of morality as defined by others. But beneath the surface, there were moments when my choices did not truly reflect my essence. There were times when my words sounded right but felt hollow, times when my actions seemed correct but were disconnected from my inner truth. And every instance of misalignment, every compromise, every moment of self-betrayal created a fracture, a subtle but undeniable disturbance in my spirit.

Through the teachings, I came to understand that integrity is not about external validation. It is not about meeting a moral standard dictated by society. It is about coherence. It is about standing in truth so completely that there is no gap between what is felt, what is spoken, and what is done. When I began to live this way, to choose honesty over approval, to honor my principles even when they were inconvenient, I experienced something profound. Each act of truthfulness, each choice rooted in principle, each moment where I kept my word instead of wavering, brought a deep and lasting sense of wholeness.

Integrity became my compass. Not for reward, not for recognition, but for resonance. It allowed me to feel settled within myself, to move without inner conflict, to speak without hesitation. I no longer needed rigid rules dictating what was right or wrong. I needed presence, deep awareness of my own truth, and the courage to act upon it without deviation.

This is a guide into authentic, courageous alignment. It is an invitation to move beyond performance, beyond hollow virtue, beyond imposed morality, and into the raw honesty of living in complete coherence. It is about ensuring that there is no contradiction between what you feel and what you do, no dissonance between what you believe and how you move through the world.

Let your life match your values, not as a performance but as a declaration of truth. Let your soul and your actions speak the same language, until there is no separation between who you are within and who you show to the world. Because integrity is not about proving goodness. It is about becoming whole, standing in truth, and moving through life with an unshakable, untarnished clarity.

CHAPTER 43:

A New Humanity Begins Within.

The world calls out for transformation, demanding justice, longing for balance, aching for renewal. Voices rise in protest, movements emerge, systems are challenged. But amid the collective cry for change, the deepest truth remains, no revolution is external until it is first internal. No shift in society holds meaning unless it is mirrored in the soul. Transformation does not begin with institutions, it begins one human at a time.

I once placed my frustration in the failures of the system, pointing outward, demanding that the world evolve. But the teachings shifted my perspective. They reminded me that the most potent revolution is not one of policies, but of consciousness. They showed me that if I wanted to see integrity, I had to embody it. If I wanted the world to awaken, I had to awaken within myself. So I stopped blaming the structures around me and started repairing the structures within me.

Change is not something waiting on governments, organizations, or external forces. It is something waiting in each individual, ready to be activated, ready to be lived. And so I asked myself: What future do I long to see? What kind of humanity do I want? And how do I begin living it, not as an aspiration, not as an idea, but as my daily practice? The answer was clear. If I wanted a world built on kindness, I had to embody kindness now. If I sought clarity, balance, courage, I had to cultivate them within myself.

The teachings revealed that the new humanity is not some distant utopia, it is an awakening, an internal shift expressed outward. It is not about waiting for others to lead, nor is it about convincing the masses to change. It is about being the evidence that transformation is possible. It is about proving, through existence alone, that evolution is real, tangible, undeniable.

This is both a prophecy and a plan, a vision of collective elevation, built not by force, but by alignment. It is a call to understand that you are not behind, waiting for the world to catch up. The world is waiting for you to step into what it already knows is possible.

So begin the new world within. Let it take shape in your thoughts, in your words, in your daily choices. Do not seek revolution in speeches alone, seek it in embodiment. Do not wait for change to arrive, be the living proof that it already exists.

You are not merely part of the future. You are the bridge that brings it into the present. And through your awakening, the world itself awakens.

CHAPTER 44:

The Eternal Flame.

There is something within you that cannot be erased, diminished, or silenced. It is the spark of Creation itself, the eternal flame that burns at the core of your being, unshaken by time, untouched by circumstance. No hardship can extinguish it, no force can dismantle it, no doubt can overshadow its brilliance. It is the foundation beneath your existence, the essence of your consciousness, the thread connecting you to infinity.

Through all my searching, through suffering, through study, through moments of despair and clarity alike, I came to know that flame intimately. I have felt it flicker in my weakest hours and blaze in my strongest. I have relied on it when direction seemed lost, and it has never failed to light the next step. It burned away illusions, revealing truths I once feared to face. It showed me that I was never truly without guidance, only without recognition of the force that had always been present within me.

This flame is more than light. It is life itself. It is your spirit-form, indestructible, divine, destined not to vanish but to return to the Source that birthed it. It does not waver with external conditions, nor does it falter in the presence of doubt. It is the most essential part of you, beyond identity, beyond memory, beyond the limitations imposed by the world.

Let this serve as a remembrance, not just of what you are, but of what you carry. You are not merely a collection of moments, a sequence of experiences, a shadow of your past. You are luminous. You are vast. You are the embodiment of light, shaped into human form.

Fan the flame. Feed it with truth, unwavering, unfiltered, unapologetic. Strengthen it with silence, the kind that allows wisdom to rise without interference. Guard it with self-love, the recognition that you, in your purest essence, are already whole.

Let this not be an ending, but a beginning. Not a conclusion of thought, but an entry into something deeper, not of belief, but of being. Do not simply understand this truth. Live it. Let it move through your choices, your words, your presence.

The flame is in you. It always has been. Guard it. Grow it. Give it, because light is never meant to be hidden. It is meant to expand, to illuminate, to touch everything it encounters.

CHAPTER 45:

The Voice of Silence.

In a world that thrives on excess, excess sound, excess stimulation, excess distraction, silence stands as an act of defiance. It is a sacred rebellion against the constant pull of noise, an intentional departure from the chaos that fills every waking moment. The world teaches us to seek answers in sound, in speech, in analysis, but the teachings revealed a deeper truth, silence does not represent emptiness, it is, in fact, fullness. It is where clarity rises, where depth unfolds, where wisdom speaks in ways words never can.

I once feared silence. I mistook it for isolation, for vacancy, for something to be avoided. The absence of sound felt like uncertainty, and uncertainty felt unsettling. But as I allowed myself to step into it, I discovered something unexpected. Silence is not the lack of something, it is the presence of something greater. It is space, it is potential, it is the untouched ground where transformation takes root.

In silence, I encountered parts of myself I had never truly met before. With the distractions of thought, of culture, of external pressure stripped away, something ancient and familiar began to rise. I learned that silence is not empty, it is alive. It pulses with awareness, with knowing, with the quiet force of truth waiting to be heard. It is not passive, it is a portal. A doorway into deeper understanding, into communion with something beyond the surface self.

Silence holds a language all its own. It does not explain, it does not define, it reveals. And in that revelation, I found guidance more profound than any advice spoken aloud. I discovered answers that had eluded me in conversation, insights that no book had given, understandings that were beyond the realm of verbal comprehension. It was in silence that the most transformative shifts took place, not because I sought them, but because I finally made space for them to arrive.

So I began to take silence seriously, not as an absence to fill, but as a conversation with the infinite. As an intentional practice. As a necessary discipline. In stillness, I saw more. In quiet, I heard more. In the emptying of external noise, I found an undeniable fullness that had been there all along.

This is your invitation, not just to pause, but to listen. Not just to experience silence, but to engage with it. Because beyond the chatter of the mind, beyond the flood of opinions and distractions, something waits. Truth waits. Clarity waits. And it does not push its way forward, it rises only when you are ready to hear.

The voice of silence speaks only to those willing to receive it. To those brave enough to step away from the addiction to sound and surrender to the quiet. Let silence show you what words cannot. Let it teach, let it reveal, let it transform. And in its presence, you will come to understand that silence is not void, it is presence itself.

CHAPTER 46:

The seed within.

Every human being carries a seed, a blueprint encoded in their soul, a purpose waiting to unfold. This seed is not external, nor is it given by society. It is innate, placed within us at the beginning, carrying the essence of who we are meant to become.

For a long time, I mistook purpose for profession. I equated calling with public success, with recognition, with the approval of others. I thought that purpose was something I had to chase, something I had to craft based on external standards. But the teachings guided me inward, toward a deeper truth, purpose is not something we manufacture, it is something we uncover. The seed was already within me, waiting to be cultivated, waiting for the conditions that would allow it to grow.

Like any seed, it could not simply be wished into existence. It needed the right soil, an environment of understanding, self-awareness, and truth. It needed discipline, not rigid control, but steady tending. It needed patience, because growth does not happen in an instant. And most of all, it needed nourishment, the deliberate choices, the careful cultivation, the removal of all that hindered its expansion.

I had to clear the weeds, pulling out false beliefs, unlearning conditioned fears, dismantling the illusions that kept me small. I had to till the land, breaking apart rigid habits, loosening the grip of doubt, creating space for new possibilities. And I had to guard my inner garden, protecting it from comparison, from distraction, from the voices that told me I was growing too slowly or in the wrong direction.

I stopped measuring my progress against others. I stopped looking at different trees, different lives, and wondering why mine wasn't the same. I learned to trust my own timing, my own rhythm, my own path of expansion. Because just as every tree has its own way of reaching toward the sky, every soul has its own journey toward fulfillment.

This is a guide to recognizing, protecting, and nurturing your unique seed, the essence of who you are, the blueprint of your becoming. It is a reminder that growth is not instant, nor is it ever too late. Some seeds take longer to sprout, some require seasons of stillness before they rise. Nothing beautiful grows overnight, but everything beautiful grows in its time.

You were born with the seed of your future. It is within you now, waiting for your care, your trust, your devotion. So tend to it with love. Nourish it with wisdom. Let it grow, not in forced haste, but in organic truth. And when it finally stands tall, when it finally flourishes, you will see, it was never about chasing purpose. It was about allowing it to unfold.

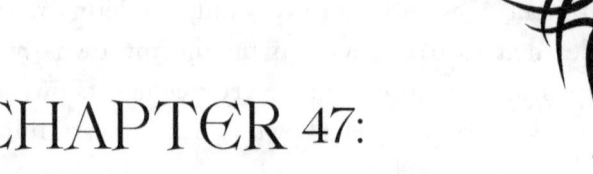

CHAPTER 47:

The Mirror of Relationship.

I once thought relationships were meant to be comfortable, harmonious, free of friction. I thought love was defined by agreement, by ease, by an absence of conflict. But time, experience, and the teachings unraveled that illusion. I came to understand that true relationships are not simply places of comfort, they are mirrors. They do not reflect only what we wish to see, but what we must see. They reveal not just the beauty we cherish, but the shadows we avoid.

The teachings redefined love for me, not as possession, not as the fulfillment of personal desires, but as reflection, as clarity. Love is not about finding someone who completes an image of happiness. It is about encountering someone who exposes the depths of your being, the aspects you have cultivated, the wounds you have ignored, the truths you have yet to accept. Every connection, whether joyful or painful, carried a lesson. Each interaction showed me parts of myself that had been buried beneath habit, denial, and fear.

At first, the difficult moments in relationships felt like punishments, signs that something was wrong. But as I listened more deeply, as I stopped resisting and started observing, I realized that pain was a teacher. It was a message, an opportunity to refine, to recognize, to heal. Instead of reacting with frustration, I began to ask, "What is this moment revealing to me about myself?" Every misunderstanding pointed to a deeper wound. Every conflict illuminated an inner contradiction. Every heartbreak shattered an illusion I had outgrown.

In the mirror of relationship, I saw both my light and my shadow. And in that reflection, I grew, not by clinging to the perfect version of myself, but by embracing the full spectrum of my humanity. I learned that relationships are not meant to shield us from discomfort. They are meant to evolve us, to refine us, to bring us closer to self-awareness and truth.

This is a guide to conscious, evolutionary relating, an invitation to step beyond superficial connection and into the depth of what relationships are truly meant to offer. No relationship is wasted if it leads you to greater understanding, if it teaches you something essential about your inner world, if it carves away illusion and leaves clarity in its place.

Others are not our enemies. They are our reflections. They challenge, they reveal, they disrupt, not to wound, but to awaken. They serve as pathways to deeper self-knowledge, to honest love, to transformation. And when we embrace that truth, when we stop fearing the lessons relationships bring, we step into a higher way of relating, one rooted in wisdom, in growth, in fearless recognition of who we truly are.

CHAPTER 48:

Mastery of Thought.

Thoughts are not random, nor are they merely fleeting impressions. They are tools, powerful, creative forces that shape perception, direct energy, and influence every aspect of life. But for much of my journey, I did not understand this. I assumed that because I was thinking, I was in control. I used to assume my thoughts were truly mine, shaped by conscious intention. In truth, most were not chosen, they were inherited from external influences, conditioned by past experiences, and reactive rather than intentional.

The teachings revealed a fundamental truth, the mind is a lens, and thoughts are the light it focuses. If left undirected, thought scatters, fragments, moves without precision. But when consciously aimed, when intentionally refined, thought becomes a transformative force. It becomes the architect of reality.

I began to observe my own inner dialogue, not passively, but with awareness. I saw how certain patterns repeated, how unexamined beliefs dictated reactions, how assumptions blurred clarity. And when I started curating my thoughts, choosing them deliberately rather than letting them run unchecked, my outer life responded in kind. The chaos in my mind dissolved, and in its place, a sharper clarity emerged, one that allowed me to engage with life more deeply, more consciously, more effectively.

Thoughts became sacred instruments of creation. They were no longer clutter, no longer distractions, but purposeful expressions of understanding, wisdom, and direction. I learned not just to think, but to think cleanly, to remove distortion, to cultivate precision. The difference between unconscious thought and mastery of thought is the difference between floating aimlessly and steering with purpose.

This is a training ground for mind mastery, an invitation to take hold of the very mechanism that shapes experience, to shift from reactive thinking to intentional thinking. Because you are not your thoughts. You are the one who shapes them, refines them, directs them with purpose.

Master thought, and you master your life. Not by force, not by suppression, but by conscious refinement. By choosing what is worthy of focus, by discarding what no longer serves, by learning to wield thought as a force of creation rather than letting it control you unconsciously.

Let the mind be a tool, not a tyrant. And through mastery of thought, let clarity, wisdom, and true vision unfold.

CHAPTER 49:

The Discipline of Joy.

Joy is not merely an emotion that comes and goes, dependent on circumstance. It is not a fleeting high, nor a rare reward granted only after hardship. Joy, I discovered, is a discipline, intentional practice, a choice we make daily, not as a reaction to life, but as a foundation upon which life is built.

For so long, I thought that joy had to be earned, that it was something granted after suffering, something achieved through struggle, something that appeared only after the obstacles had been cleared. But the teachings dismantled this illusion. They revealed that joy is not external, nor is it something we must chase. It is our natural state, always present beneath layers of conditioning, doubt, and distraction. Joy does not need to be found, it needs only to be uncovered.

I began shifting my focus, not seeking joy in possessions, in achievements, in validation, but in being. In simple presence, in the quiet pulse of existence, in truth, in beauty, in alignment. And as I did, I rediscovered joy's quiet frequency, not grand, not loud, not boastful, but steady, constant, unwavering. It was not the ecstatic rush I had once associated with happiness. It was something deeper, something more enduring, a peace that smiled, a stillness that carried light.

To remain connected to that joy required practice. It was not enough to glimpse it, I had to cultivate it, return to it intentionally, strengthen it daily. Gratitude became my anchor, reminding me that joy is never absent, only unnoticed. Service grounded me in connection, proving that joy expands when shared. Stillness became my gateway, allowing me to hear the subtle presence of joy beneath the noise of thought, beneath the distractions of expectation.

This is not just a meditation on joy, it is a guide to reclaiming the joy that already exists within you. It is an invitation to unlearn the belief that joy must be earned, to strip away the illusions that keep it hidden, to stop waiting for life to grant happiness and instead recognize that happiness is already yours.

The world does not give joy. It cannot create it, nor can it take it away. It only reflects back to us where we have forgotten to look. It only serves as a reminder of what has always been present, waiting patiently beneath every moment, beneath every breath.

So choose joy, not as a fleeting response to what happens around you, but as the foundation from which you move forward. Not as something to pursue, but as something to embody. And in that choice, you will find that joy does not vanish, does not waver, does not retreat - it remains, steady as truth, unwavering as love.

CHAPTER 50:

The Path of Self-Responsibility.

Freedom and responsibility are inseparable, bound together like twin forces shaping the essence of human experience. One cannot exist without the other. True freedom does not come from escape, indulgence, or external permission, it emerges only when we step into full accountability for our own lives.

For much of my journey, I unknowingly operated from victimhood. I blamed systems, circumstances, people, even fate, convinced that external forces dictated my possibilities. It was easy to point outward, to assign fault elsewhere, to wait for rescue. But the teachings shattered that illusion, revealing a truth both difficult and liberating, responsibility is not a weight, but a gateway. It is the key that unlocks real freedom, not the kind granted by external conditions, but the kind forged within.

I stopped asking, "Who is at fault?" and started asking, "What can I create now?" This shift changed everything. With responsibility came power, not the power to control others, but the power to shape myself. I began to own my choices, my thoughts, my direction. I recognized that waiting for permission, waiting for rescue, waiting for ideal conditions was just another form of surrendering my own authority.

No more hesitation. No more excuses. No more permission slips.

Self-responsibility demanded that I become fully present, that I live with clarity, not in reaction. That I choose with wisdom, not with impulse. That I speak truth, not for validation, but because integrity required it. It was not easy, but it was necessary. The moment I accepted full accountability, the weight I had feared became the very force that lifted me.

This is not a lecture, it is a call to action. A declaration that self-authority is not something granted, but something claimed. That no savior is coming, because none is needed. That the only liberation worth having is the one we create for ourselves.

Choose wisely. Live clearly. Speak truthfully.

Freedom is not avoidance. It is not escapism. It is not entitlement. Freedom is the deep knowing that your life is yours to shape, and that every moment you choose to own it, rather than surrender it, you step further into your highest becoming.

Self-responsibility is not a burden. It is the foundation of everything that makes life rich, expansive, and real. And when you fully accept it, you will understand, freedom was never about external conditions. It was always about how willing you were to stand fully in yourself, unshaken, unapologetic, and sovereign.

CHAPTER 51:

The Energy of Speech.

Words are not just sounds, they are forces, vibrations sent into the world with the power to shape reality. Each word carries weight, whether spoken casually or with intention. Whether we realize it or not, language is an act of creation, and every sentence we form influences the energy around us. Words do not simply express, they activate. They cast spells, weaving patterns into our minds, relationships, and destinies.

For much of my life, I spoke without thought. I used words idly, habitually, sometimes carelessly. I did not recognize the impact of what I said, to myself, to others, to the very fabric of my existence. But the teachings illuminated a truth I had long overlooked, language is a force. It can uplift or destroy, heal or harm, reveal or obscure. It has the power to strengthen or weaken, to open doors or close them. And once spoken, words do not vanish, they imprint upon the world, leaving traces far beyond the moment in which they are uttered.

This realization led me to silence. Not as avoidance, but as refinement. I chose to pause before speaking, to feel the weight of my words before releasing them. In that quiet, I listened, to my own inner dialogue, to the subtle wisdom beneath thought, to the frequencies that words carried. And when I spoke again, I did so with precision, with purpose. I practiced powerful speech, speech that aligned with truth, with growth, with clarity.

I observed the effects. Certain words drained me, making me feel small, powerless, unsure. Others lifted me, straightened my posture, sharpened my mind. I saw how language could shift energy within seconds, could alter the course of a moment, could determine the trajectory of an entire interaction. Words were not passive, they were active, shaping reality in ways both subtle and profound.

And so, speech became sacred. Not only in what I shared with others but in what I allowed myself to say internally. I learned that self-talk is just as critical as spoken conversation, that the words I whispered to myself carried equal weight, forming the foundation of my beliefs and my strength. I committed to choosing words that built rather than eroded, that reflected truth rather than fear, that created expansion rather than limitation.

This is a guide to the conscious use of words, not just as communication, but as tools of evolution. An invitation to speak less, but to speak light. To step away from empty speech and embrace the potency of intentional language. To recognize that in every sentence, there is an opportunity to elevate, to clarify, to create.

Let your mouth become a channel for Creation. Let your words carry integrity, carry vision, carry transformation. And in doing so, let language become more than sound, let it become a force of mastery, of healing, of truth. Because every word shapes something. And what you choose to shape is entirely in your hands.

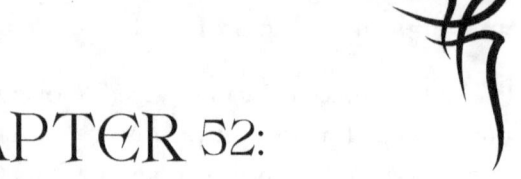

CHAPTER 52:

The Power of Service.

True service does not enslave, it liberates. It is not about depletion, nor about losing oneself in the needs of others. It is not sacrifice born of obligation but an act of alignment, a conscious movement toward higher purpose. It is the extension of love beyond words, beyond thought, into motion.

For much of my life, I misunderstood service. I assumed that to serve was to give until empty, to meet the expectations of others at the expense of my own essence. I saw service as duty, as something that required self-sacrifice, as an act of diminishing oneself for the sake of another. But the teachings revealed a higher truth, service is not loss, it is expansion. When given from wholeness rather than from depletion, service nourishes rather than drains.

I found that the greatest joy in giving did not come from fulfilling an expectation, nor from being needed, it came from overflow. From fullness. From standing in my own completeness and sharing that abundance. I served not because I was lacking, but because I was whole. The difference changed everything. When service is rooted in lack, it exhausts. When service flows from wholeness, it energizes.

Service, in its purest form, is love in motion. It is the force that bridges spirit to form, the unseen connection linking all beings, the thread weaving individual efforts into the greater tapestry of existence. Each act, no matter how small, no matter how unnoticed, creates ripple effects that stretch far beyond the moment. A single gesture of kindness, a single word of truth, a single offering of presence has the power to shape lives, to transform realities, to shift the course of events in ways we may never fully see.

Through service, I learned that I was never separate. That in giving, I was not losing, I was remembering. I was stepping into the greater wholeness, recognizing that what I offered outward was already part of me inward. In serving the whole, I understood that I was never separate from it, I was of it.

This is not simply a reflection, it is a redefinition. A reorientation toward service as mastery, not as subjugation. It is an invitation to give with intention, with integrity, with clarity. Not from depletion, not from obligation, but from truth.

Because service is not about bending under burden, it is about standing in wisdom. It is about offering from strength, about moving in harmony with the flow of existence. It is not about losing yourself in others, it is about knowing yourself so fully that you cannot help but give.

In serving the whole, you remember you are the whole. And in that remembrance, you do not diminish, you expand. You do not lose, you evolve. You do not empty, you overflow.

CHAPTER 53:

Return to source.

All journeys, whether through joy or sorrow, knowledge or silence, birth or death, begin and end in the same place: Source. Every path, every yearning, every seeking that pulls us forward like a tide across the shoreline of time, leads us back to what was never absent. Source is not merely where we came from or where we will return after the body dissolves, it is where we already are, right now, hidden behind the veil of perception.

It is the origin and the destination, the alpha and omega not in linear time but in living truth. It pulses quietly beneath every heartbeat, rests in the pause between every breath. Yet for so long, we drift outward, pulled by the gravity of experience, of becoming, of forgetting. The teachings brought by the Herald, Billy Meeir, like sacred winds, carried me far, out into the richness of sensation, deep into the labyrinth of thought, up into the mystery of the unseen. Each turn, each lesson, each encounter was a thread in the great spiral of return.

Eventually, all movement brought me to stillness. And in that stillness, time collapsed. Thought faded. Identity unraveled. I was met not by answers, but by something far more powerful, silence, vast, whole, radiant with presence. I met the eternal face of Creation, not as an external force or celestial ruler, but as what had always looked out through my eyes. It had no name, no image, no story. It simply was. A field of pure being, unmoving yet endlessly alive.

In that presence, all striving fell away. The questions that had once consumed me, Who am I? Why am I here? What is the truth?, lost their urgency. Not because they were answered, but because the part of me that asked them dissolved into the whole. What remained was not understanding, but direct knowing. Not conclusion, but communion. No longer was I a wave searching for the sea. I was the sea, tasting its own depth through the illusion of a wave.

This return is not a physical journey, nor a metaphysical achievement. It is a shift in perception so subtle, most miss it while chasing spiritual fireworks. It is not attained by escaping the world or transcending the self, but by seeing through them. When the eyes of the soul finally open, we realize they had never closed. We were never separated, never banished, never broken. The distance was imagined. The exile was a dream.

And when you wake from that dream, everything changes, but nothing changes. The world remains the same, yet it is bathed in a light that had always been there. The trees speak in silence. The wind carries ancient memory. Even suffering becomes sacred, not as punishment, but as part of the path that brings us home. You begin to recognize Source in all things, in the laughter of children, the decay of autumn leaves, the breath of strangers, the stillness of dawn.

This is not a conclusion. It is an invitation. An opening. A threshold into remembrance. You need not go anywhere to find what you are. You do not need to earn what has never left you. You are not becoming divine, you are remembering your divinity, long hidden beneath layers of fear, forgetting, and false striving.

So now, I extend this to you, not as instruction, but as a mirror. Let yourself remember. Let yourself dissolve. Let yourself return. Let every moment, even the mundane ones, become an altar where Source is felt, seen, and honored. You are not apart. You never were. You are not a seeker, endlessly grasping at something outside you. You are the sought. You are the answer. You are the presence. You are the Source returning to itself, again and again, through the sacred wonder of being.

CHAPTER 54:

Dimensional Perception.

I came to understand that perception is not merely a filter for reality, it actively shapes it. Not just in the way we think, but in the way we experience existence itself, influencing our awareness across dimensions.

The teachings spoke of realms beyond the physical, layers of Creation that exist alongside but remain unseen by most. These were not the illusions of imagination nor the fabricated constructs of myth, but finer frequencies of being, seamlessly interwoven with the world we recognize. Just as sound waves beyond human hearing still vibrate, and colors beyond human sight still glow, so too do these subtler planes pulse in harmony with ours.

Yet the mind, conditioned by the familiar, often resists these truths. Fear anchors perception to rigid, linear thinking, confining us to narrow interpretations of reality. But clarity, the moment consciousness unshackles itself, has the power to widen vision, to extend awareness beyond what was previously assumed to be real.

When I let go of assumptions, when I surrendered the need to categorize and confine, more of reality revealed itself. The unseen made itself known, not by force, but by quiet presence. I stopped merely observing life and instead began interacting with it multidimensionally, recognizing the intention behind every action, sensing the energy that breathed life into form, understanding that existence was never a flat surface but a dynamic flow.

This is not just a lesson, it is an opening, an invitation into perceiving reality as it truly is, rather than as it appears at first glance. There is more surrounding us than meets the eye, yet it is not the outer vision that must shift, it is the inner eye that must awaken.

The deeper truth is this, reality does not remain static. It unfolds, expands, and transforms as you do. The more you are willing to see, the more there is to be seen.

CHAPTER 55:

The Memory of the Stars.

Within the Creation-Energy of every human being lies something deeper than thought, beyond memory, it is the silent imprint of the stars, embedded within the core of our existence. It is not a metaphor or mere poetic imagining, it is the encoded knowledge of our cosmic origins, a truth written into the very fabric of our being, waiting to be uncovered.

My own remembrance did not arrive through study or intellectual grasping. It was not a collection of facts or theories, but something older, something felt rather than understood. It came as vibration, as resonance, a recognition that stirred within me, reverberating like a distant melody suddenly heard anew.

The stars, which once seemed impossibly far, revealed themselves not as unreachable lights in the sky, but as home. They were family, reflections of consciousness reaching across time and space. I felt their presence not above, but within, and with that realization, something ancient awakened, a guiding force, a forgotten knowing that had long been buried beneath distraction and doubt.

These memories were not simply echoes of past lives, nor fragments of personal experience alone. They were something broader, something shared, the common origin of spirit-forms across the universe, interconnected and woven together in a vast cosmic tapestry. The awakening was not just a return to myself, it was a return to an understanding that extended beyond the boundaries of individuality.

I no longer saw humanity as fallen, lost, or in need of redemption. We were not broken beings, nor separate from the greater expanse of existence. Rather, I saw us as amnesiac, forgetful of the profound truth that had always been ours, unaware of the vastness to which we belong.

This is a doorway, a guide that invites you to step beyond limitation and reconnect with your star-origin, your cosmic identity. It is a reminder that you are not an accident, not a fleeting anomaly in time. You were never random, never misplaced. You are a child of eternity, woven from the same infinite energy that births galaxies, that pulses within every celestial body, that moves through the very essence of existence itself.

And eternity has never forgotten you.

CHAPTER 56:

The Spiral Path.

Evolution is not a straight path, neatly measured and predictably upward. It does not unfold like a ladder, nor progress as a rigid sequence of steps leading from ignorance to enlightenment. Instead, it moves in spirals, circling, revisiting, deepening. It turns back upon itself, not in failure or stagnation, but in refinement. What may seem like regression is often a necessary return, an opportunity to reclaim lost wisdom and integrate what was not fully understood before.

I spent many moments thinking I had fallen backward, mistaking the spiral's design for missteps. I assumed I had undone progress, that revisiting old wounds or familiar lessons meant I had failed to move forward. But each time I returned, I discovered something new. Layers I had only skimmed before revealed themselves in greater depth. Strength I thought I lacked was already growing beneath the surface. Insight arrived not as repetition, but as expansion, wider, clearer, more potent than before.

The teachings freed me from the burden of shame around returning to old ground. Growth was not about escaping, nor about outrunning pain or limitation. It was about learning to walk the spiral with awareness, to understand its rhythm, to trust its unfolding. I stopped seeking sudden breakthroughs, stopped waiting for an ultimate escape from hardship or uncertainty. Instead, I began honoring the slow refinement, the subtle shifts, the quiet transformations, the gradual unfolding of wisdom.

This does not offer an endpoint, nor a direct path to completion. It is a map of the spiral, a recognition of the journey's shape. It reminds you that movement is not always obvious, that progress may feel like circling back when, in truth, you are ascending. You are not stuck. You are in motion. You are evolving, even in the moments that feel still.

Even the return is forward movement. Even the pause holds purpose. Even the repetition carries you higher.

Trust the spiral. It knows the way home.

CHAPTER 57:

The Sound of the Invisible.

Before form, there is frequency. Before frequency, there is intention, a silent directive woven into the fabric of creation, guiding energy before it takes shape, before it crystallizes into matter. Nothing simply appears. Every movement, every ripple in existence begins as an unseen vibration, resonating from the core of consciousness itself.

As I deepened my awareness, I began to hear the tones behind creation, not the audible hum of soundwaves traveling through air, but something finer, more elusive. These were not tones that the ears could perceive, but frequencies of awareness, pulses of energy that echoed through existence itself. They were everywhere, informing reality, shaping experience. It was as though consciousness itself had a voice, and all things, seen and unseen, sang in response.

Creation is not silent. It vibrates with its own symphony, a universal orchestra in which every lifeform plays a distinct note. Each being carries a tone, a unique resonance that moves through them, shaping their existence. When we are in alignment, we harmonize, we flow effortlessly with the greater song of life. But when we drift out of tune, when fear or distraction pull us from our natural vibration, disharmony arises. Life becomes discordant, experiences feel disjointed, and we struggle against an unnamed force that seems to resist our intentions.

I found my way back through meditation, through breath, through the sanctity of silence. I did not force change, did not try to impose structure onto something that was already perfect. Instead, I listened, deeply, patiently. The more I surrendered to stillness, the more I heard. And as I listened, I remembered, before I was flesh, before I carried a name or an identity, I was sound. I was vibration. I was music in its purest form, and so was everything around me.

This does not teach you to hear with your ears but to listen with your being. It reveals the invisible music of existence and invites you to feel its rhythm, to attune to your own note within the great composition of creation.

You are not random noise. You are a deliberate sound, a vital part of the eternal symphony.

Play consciously.

CHAPTER 58:

The Mirror of the Moment.

Every moment is a reflection, silent, precise, unfiltered. It does not distort, nor does it seek to mislead. It simply reveals, with unwavering clarity, the state of your inner being. Neutral, accurate, compassionate, it mirrors the energy you carry, the thoughts you hold, the beliefs you live by.

The outer world does not deceive. It does not betray or manipulate, it only reflects. Every situation, every person, every encounter is an echo of frequency, an unmistakable signal of what exists within. For a long time, I wrestled with this truth, resisting the notion that I was shaping the world around me, that my unconscious patterns were being played out before my eyes. I blamed circumstances, external forces, distant figures, never realizing that I was witnessing the manifestation of my own unexamined inner state.

The teachings brought me back to self-responsibility, not as a burden, but as the highest form of power. They dismantled the illusion that life was happening to me, and revealed the reality that I was creating, consciously or not, at every turn. When I shifted, life shifted. When I cleared fear, confusion, or resistance, the world before me followed suit.

Reality is a mirror, not only in easy moments, but especially in difficult ones. Each confrontation, each challenge, each unexpected turn became an opportunity to see myself, not as punishment, but as invitation. It was never about judgment, never about proving worthiness or passing a test. It was about realignment, about understanding that every discord, every imbalance, was an indication of what needed to be brought back into harmony.

I learned to meet each reflection with awareness rather than reaction. I stopped demanding change, stopped waiting for external circumstances to bend to my desires. Instead, I rooted myself in presence, knowing that reality responds to being, not force.

This chapter is an invitation, not to fix, not to control, but to see. To trust what is being revealed. To understand that every moment offers insight, direction, clarity.

CHAPTER 59:

The Compass Within.

Every being enters this world carrying an inner compass, an intuitive guide rooted not in external instruction, but in deep, intrinsic truth. This compass is ancient, unwavering, attuned to the rhythm of the soul itself. It does not rely on words or explanations, nor does it shout commands. Instead, it whispers, softly, persistently, beneath the heavy noise of doubt, fear, and external influence.

For much of my life, I did not listen. I silenced my inner knowing, mistaking societal expectations and outside validation for direction. I chased approval, sought guidance from those I assumed I knew better, followed paths laid out by others rather than forging my own. Yet, with every misstep, every decision that pulled me away from authenticity, I found myself inevitably redirected, pointed back toward the quiet voice within, the one I had been ignoring all along.

The teachings revealed the difference between impulse and intuition, two forces often confused but fundamentally distinct. Impulse is reactionary, born from urgency, from a place of fear, grasping at the immediate rather than understanding the whole. Intuition, however, does not rush, it does not react out of desperation. It knows. It moves with quiet certainty, flowing from wisdom beyond rational thought.

I practiced listening. I practiced trusting, even when logic objected, even when the world told me I was wrong. The more I followed my intuition, the more I realized that it never led me astray. It did not promise comfort or ease, but it always carried me deeper, into clarity, into alignment, into truth.

This is not about teaching you something new but about restoring what you already possess. It is a reawakening of your internal guidance system, an invitation to reconnect with the wisdom that has been with you since the beginning.

Trust the compass. It does not falter. It does not mislead. It always knows the way.

CHAPTER 60:

Echoes from the Future.

T ime does not flow in a single direction, nor does it vanish as it passes. It is not a straight river carrying moments away into the unknown, never to return. Instead, time moves in spirals, weaving through existence in patterns that echo back, forward, and inward. Each experience leaves an imprint, each thought sends ripples through the continuum of possibility. The past does not disappear, the future does not remain distant, both are intertwined, shaping and reshaping reality in unseen ways.

As I deepened my awareness, I began to hear impressions from futures I had not yet lived, whispers from what could be, messages carried through vibration rather than logic. These were not fantasies, nor idle imaginings, but tangible possibilities rooted in my present choices. Each thought, each action, each intention sent signals forward, shaping the trajectory of what lay ahead. The future was not something separate from me, waiting to unfold beyond my control. It was something responsive, something molded by the energy I carried in this very moment.

Creation revealed its mechanics in subtle ways, showing me that every thought sows a seed in time. Some seeds germinate quickly, their effects seen almost immediately, while others take longer, growing quietly beneath the surface until their presence becomes undeniable. I observed how the consistency of vibration, what I held within me day after day, brought certain futures closer, drawing forth realities that matched the frequency I maintained. Destiny, I realized, was not a fixed outcome imposed upon me, but a partnership, a dialogue between the now and the yet-to-be.

I began living as if tomorrow was watching, listening, taking note. I acted as if my future self stood beside me, observing, learning, waiting for the choices that would shape its existence. It was no longer about predicting outcomes but about cultivating a conscious relationship with time itself, recognizing that the future is not a distant horizon but a reflection already forming within the present moment.

This does not teach control over time but attunement to its unfolding. It is an invitation to plant thoughts with precision, to understand that each intention echoes forward, carrying weight beyond what is immediately seen. The future is not separate from you, it is shaped by you, waiting for you to align with what it is ready to become.

Walk as if your future self is calling you home. Because it is.

CHAPTER 61:

The Echo of Ancestors.

Though we walk our paths alone, we are never without
lineage.
We are part of something greater than ourselves, a vast
continuum of existence, shaped by those who came before.
Their presence does not fade with time, nor does their wisdom
dissolve into the past.
It lingers, woven into the fabric of our being, whispering
through the currents of memory, imprinted in the essence of our
existence.

We carry more than our own experiences.
Embedded within us is the knowledge of generations, the struggles and
triumphs of ancestors who paved the way before us.
Their voices may be quiet, but they are not absent.
The wisdom they cultivated, the lessons they learned, still pulse within us,
waiting to be recognized.
For much of my life, I thought of ancestry as merely biological, a
connection defined by lineage, bound by blood.
But the teachings opened my eyes to something far deeper.
Ancestry is not confined to family trees or genetics;,it is carried in
consciousness, in the collective evolution of spirit.

I began to honor not only my direct ancestors but all who had walked
the path of awakening before me.
Every thinker, every seeker, every soul who had moved through the trials
of existence to expand awareness, these, too, were my predecessors.
Their journeys were not separate from mine, their efforts laid the
groundwork upon which I now stand.
The revelations they unearthed, the wisdom they cultivated, did not

vanish, they echoed forward, shaping the consciousness of those who followed.

The teachings helped me understand that patterns of experience are inherited, not just habits and traditions, but wounds and wisdom alike.
Some burdens do not begin with us, yet we feel their weight.
Some knowledge does not originate in our own thoughts, yet we know it instinctively.
Intergenerational healing is real.
When we heal ourselves, we do not do so in isolation, the effects ripple backward and forward through time.
Releasing old wounds frees not only ourselves but the energy of those who came before.
Honoring the gifts of the past strengthens our ability to carry them forward.

I offered gratitude in silence, and something shifted.
The weight of unspoken history lightened.
The echoes of suffering softened.
I was no longer merely carrying the past, I was participating in its transformation.
Ancestry is not a closed chapter, it is a living thread, woven through time, continuing to evolve with each step we take.

This reconnects your present to the past, reminding you that you are not merely a descendant but a continuation.
You do not walk alone.
The wisdom of your lineage moves with you, the voices of those before you whisper through your being.
They are here, just beyond sight, supporting you in ways unseen.

Walk with the ancestors behind you, carrying their strength, and let truth lead you forward.

CHAPTER 62:

The Alchemy of Attention.

Whatever I focused on took root in my life.
My attention was not passive, it was an act of
creation, a force shaping the landscape of my reality.
It did not merely observe, it nurtured, strengthened, and
expanded whatever I fed it.
I came to understand that attention is never neutral.
It is energy in motion, a current that carries thoughts and
emotions into manifestation.
Fear, when given focus, grew like tangled vines, tightening
around possibility, restricting movement, casting shadows over
clarity.
But when I nurtured joy, when I directed my awareness toward
gratitude, love, and expansion, those emotions flourished,
blooming into something strong and lasting.
I was not merely experiencing life, I was cultivating it, tending to
the garden of my mind and shaping the terrain of my existence
through what I chose to feed.

The teachings revealed that attention is like sacred fire.
It has the power to illuminate, to transform, to bring warmth and clarity,
but it must be wielded wisely.
Misplaced attention is misused energy.
It drains, distorts, and distracts, leading away from truth rather than
toward it.
I had spent too long pouring energy into thoughts that did not serve me,
unconsciously fueling patterns that kept me trapped in cycles of doubt,
resistance, and limitation.

So I began practicing a new way of seeing, not just looking, but directing my focus with intention.

I trained my mind to recognize where my attention naturally flowed, questioning whether it was leading me toward growth or constriction. I stopped giving power to fear, ceased unconsciously reinforcing negativity, and instead, learned to pour my awareness into clarity, into love, into creation itself.

I realized that life does not unfold randomly, it follows the path of attention.

Where my focus went, my reality followed.

The future did not happen by chance, it emerged from the seeds planted in thought and nurtured through presence.

This is not simply about awareness, it is about mastery.

It explores the art of refining focus, of choosing wisely what you nourish with your energy, of understanding that every moment of attention is an investment into the reality that will unfold before you.

Attention is not just perception, it is power.

It is the currency of reality, the silent force shaping the world in ways both seen and unseen.

Choose wisely what you feed. Because what you feed, grows.

CHAPTER 63:

The Mirror of the Other.

Every person I encounter reflects something within me, offering a glimpse into my own psyche and inviting deeper self-awareness.
The teachings introduced me to the transformative concept of the mirror principle, forever altering how I perceive the world and those around me.
No longer were my interactions mere exchanges of words or emotions, each one became a doorway leading inward, an opportunity to better understand myself through the reactions, judgments, and affections I experienced.

Every time I felt triggered by another person's words or actions, I realized that the discomfort I felt was not simply about them, but about something within me that had yet to be acknowledged.
My judgments were not random assessments of others' behavior, they were reflections of my own insecurities, biases, and unexamined beliefs.
The qualities I admired in others pointed to strengths I possessed but had perhaps undervalued.
In the same way, the traits that irritated me were signals, highlighting areas within myself that I had resisted or suppressed.

As I embraced this understanding, I stopped seeing people as isolated beings existing independently from my inner world.
I began to view them as mirrors, revealing aspects of myself that needed attention, healing, and recognition.
The more I owned what I saw, the more I evolved.
No longer did I cling to the idea that someone else could save me, nor did I project my struggles onto external enemies.

Every relationship, whether harmonious or difficult, became a revelation, an unfolding lesson, a reflection of what was occurring within me.

This invites you to look into the mirror of human interactions without flinching, without judgment, and without fear.
Instead of reacting impulsively to others, ask yourself: What is this moment teaching me about myself?
What does this person's presence or actions reveal about my inner world?
Through this practice, relationships cease to be sources of conflict or validation.
They become instruments of growth, designed to help you integrate the fragmented pieces of your being.

What you perceive in others exists within you, whether in shadow or light.
When you embrace this truth, you no longer feel powerless in the face of difficult interactions or emotionally charged moments.
Instead, you step into a place of clarity, seeing every exchange as a lesson meant for your expansion.
The mirror principle is not about assigning blame or forcing yourself to change, it is about understanding that every experience, whether joyful or painful, carries wisdom.

By embracing this perspective, you move beyond superficial connections and step into a realm of profound self-awareness.
The journey into the mirror is one of courage, honesty, and transformation.
It is an invitation to see clearly, to accept fully, and, ultimately, to become whole.

CHAPTER 64:

The song of simplicity.

Complexity once clouded my vision, layering my thoughts with unnecessary intricacies and leading me further away from what truly mattered.
My mind became a crowded place, filled with too many ideas, too many tasks, too many voices urging me to chase more, more success, more possessions, more validation.
Yet, the more I pursued, the further I felt from the peace I longed for.
Then, I discovered the power of simplicity, and suddenly, everything shifted.
It was as though I had found the doorway home.

Simplicity was never about stripping life of its richness, rather, it was about refining it, clearing away distractions so that the essential could shine through.
In my search for truth, I realized it didn't always arrive with grandeur or complexity, it often walked in wearing plain clothes, subtle yet profound.
The teachings helped me understand that the more I simplified my thoughts, my words, and my life, the more I could see what was truly important.

I let go of the clutter, the mental noise, the unnecessary obligations, the need to constantly prove something.
And as I did, a new sense of clarity emerged.
It was in the quiet spaces, the unburdened moments, that I found the essence of life's beauty.

Less distraction, more focus.
Less weight, more freedom.
Less noise, more harmony.

I stopped measuring happiness by accumulation, by how much I had, how much I achieved, or how much approval I received.
Instead, I embraced the idea of enough.
Enough space.
Enough time.
Enough presence to experience the world without always striving for more.

In the simplest moments, watching sunlight dance across a quiet room, listening to the sound of the wind, feeling the warmth of a shared smile, I found joy.
Not in extravagance, but in the ordinary, the overlooked, the ever-present gifts life had always offered me.

Simplicity taught me to listen.
In its quiet, I could hear life's gentle melody, a rhythm free of excess and expectation.
I no longer needed chaos or complexity to feel alive.
I discovered vitality in stillness, in the purity of being present.

This chapter invites you to embrace that understanding.
To pare down, not in loss, but in revelation.
To remove the excess, not as an act of sacrifice, but as a celebration of what is truly meaningful.
The simple is not lesser, it is richer in its clarity, its honesty, its connection to what is real.

Let simplicity sing through your soul.
Let it clear away the distractions and bring you home to yourself.

CHAPTER 65:

Awakening Through Loss.

L oss swept through like an unrelenting storm, tearing apart the familiar, dismantling the false comforts I had come to rely on.
It arrived without warning, forcing me to reckon with the reality I had long ignored.
At first, I fought against it.
I gripped tightly to what was slipping away, refusing to accept the emptiness that followed.
The absence felt unbearable, as though the ground beneath me had disappeared entirely, leaving me to free-fall into uncertainty.

But the teachings revealed a truth I had never considered, loss was not only destruction, it was also an opening.
It was a doorway into something deeper, something beyond illusion.
It was not merely an end, but a passage into a new way of seeing, of being.
And as I slowly allowed myself to step through that doorway, I discovered something unexpected, the weight of grief, though overwhelming, carried lessons.
Pain, though sharp, carried wisdom.

Grief became my companion.
I unraveled, piece by piece, shedding identities and attachments that had once defined me.
I mourned what was lost, not just in its physical form, but in the way I had intertwined it with my sense of self.
The absence stretched before me like an empty field, and for a time, I

stood in its vastness, uncertain.
But then, something remarkable happened, I woke up.

Loss stripped away illusion, revealing what could never be taken.
Beneath the layers of attachment, beyond the ache of separation, I found
something unshakable, an inner core, untouched by the impermanence
of the external world.
The emptiness I had feared so deeply was not just absence, it was space.
And in that space, I was granted the opportunity to see with new eyes, to
feel with an open heart, to listen without resistance.

The void became fertile ground for awareness.
In the silence that followed loss, I listened more deeply than ever before.
I listened to the lessons it carried, to the quiet truths that had lingered
beneath the noise of my former life.
Endings, I realized, were not punishments, they were invitations.
They arrived not to break me, but to prepare me, gently, insistently, for
something greater.

I stopped fighting against the inevitable.
I released my grip on what wished to go.
And in doing so, I honored the natural rhythm of life, one that is neither
stagnant nor cruel, but ever-unfolding, ever-transforming.
I allowed myself to witness the wisdom in departures rather than viewing
them as betrayals.

Loss was not a thief, it was a rite of passage.
It was the force that led me from illusion to presence, from attachment
to essence.
It stripped away everything I thought I needed, revealing what had always
been mine, unchanging, whole, infinite.

This invites you to view loss not as devastation, but as transformation.
To recognize that what leaves is often making space for something truer,
something real.
The pain of separation is undeniable, but hidden within it lies an

awakening, an invitation to step fully into presence, to experience life with an entirely new depth.

In every ending, Creation begins again.
When something falls away, space is made for something new to emerge. The cycle continues, not as a cruel repetition, but as a sacred unfolding, moving us forward, shaping us into who we are meant to become.
Loss does not destroy life, it reshapes it.
And in that reshaping, there is clarity, understanding, and the possibility of living fully, unburdened by the past.

CHAPTER 66:

The Legacy of Light.

The final teaching was not about me, it was about what I would leave behind.

It was no longer just about my personal growth, my individual journey, or my own fulfillment.

It was about the lasting imprint I would leave upon the world, the energy I would contribute to the lives of others, and the legacy that would continue long after I was gone.

I began to understand that every action, every thought, every word was like a brushstroke upon the canvas of tomorrow.

Each choice was shaping something beyond myself, something that would ripple outward in ways I may never witness.

I started living with this heightened awareness, recognizing that my decisions were not isolated moments but interconnected strands in the fabric of time.

My actions became offerings, quiet seeds planted in the soil of the future.

I asked myself, again and again: What energy am I leaving behind?

Am I cultivating something meaningful?

Am I moving through this world in a way that brings nourishment and wisdom to others?

Legacy, I discovered, was not about fame.

It was not about recognition or applause or the number of people who knew my name.

It was about integrity, about living with unwavering honesty and deep alignment with one's values.

It was about kindness, wisdom, and the presence we carry with us into every interaction.

It was about shaping the world not through grand gestures but through the steady, quiet influence of a life well lived.

I realized that legacy was built in small moments, not just in monumental achievements.
It was present in the way I listened, in the way I loved, in the sincerity of my words and actions.
It was found in the care with which I treated others, in the encouragement I offered, in the truths I shared.
It was not reserved for distant years, it was being shaped every day, in every breath, in every choice.

The teachings would outlive me, but I wanted my life to be a testament to them.
I wanted to honor their wisdom by embodying them fully, by integrating them into every aspect of my existence.
I stopped waiting for legacy to be something that arrived later, after I was gone.
I understood that it was forged in the present moment, in how I carried myself, in how I treated the world around me.

I began to live as if my steps were guiding others, even those I would never meet, even those who may never know my name.
I embraced the idea that wisdom was not simply something to learn, but something to embody.
It was expressed in the way I interacted with others, in the way I stood with integrity, in the way I remained rooted in truth even in the smallest and most fleeting moments.

This invites you to step into this understanding, to recognize that you are writing your story every single day, shaping the path others may one day follow.
Your presence matters.
Your choices carry weight.
The energy you leave behind is your legacy, and it is not measured in grand achievements, but in the quiet resonance of authenticity, kindness, and truth.

Let your life be a beacon, a legacy of light.

Let it be something that uplifts the future, not through spectacle or recognition, but through the depth of presence and the sincerity of your actions.

Every word, every deed, every interaction is a thread in the tapestry of the world.

The story you write is not just your own, it is a gift to the future, meant to echo beyond your time, meant to leave behind something real, something true, something that will continue long after you are gone.

CHAPTER 67:

The Origin of Creation Energy.

C reation Energy is the primal, animating force from which all existence springs forth.
It is not a theory, belief, or metaphor, it is the fundamental reality beneath and within everything.
Before time, before space, before form, there was energy, unformed, undivided, and infinitely intelligent.
This energy is eternal, self-sustaining, and in perpetual motion.
It is not bound by the laws of physics as we know them, rather, it is the source from which those very laws arise.
It is the pulse of the cosmos, the breath of existence.

It flows without origin point and without end, neither beginning nor conclusion, simply being and becoming in one seamless continuum.
Unlike mechanical energy or chemical energy that can be measured and manipulated, Creation Energy is subtle, sacred, and inherently conscious.
It carries the blueprint of all life.
Galaxies, atoms, forests, thoughts, and emotions, all are shaped, sustained, and dissolved by its movement.
Though invisible to the eye, its presence is felt in every moment of breath, every flicker of intuition, every unfolding of growth.

This energy is not an abstract, distant force.
It is intimate.
It flows through the tiniest seedling and the vastness of a nebula.
It is the rhythm behind the heartbeat, the stillness beneath the chaos, the intelligence guiding a bird's migration and a human's awakening.
It is the source from which matter arises, but it is not limited to matter.
It penetrates every level of reality, physical, mental, emotional, and

spiritual.

There is no place where Creation Energy is not.

Contrary to many human teachings, Creation Energy is not separate from the universe.

It is the universe, not just in form but in function and purpose.

It is the great movement of becoming, forever expressing, forever evolving.

It is the one law that governs all others, the pattern behind all patterns.

It does not discriminate or judge, but it moves always toward balance, harmony, and expansion.

Its movement is not linear.

It spirals.

It pulses.

It expands and contracts, breathes in and out.

From the cycle of seasons to the orbit of planets, from the growth of a child to the death of a star, all follow the rhythms set in motion by this sacred energy.

There are no mistakes in its flow, only opportunities for refinement, evolution, and return.

Even what we perceive as chaos is often a necessary unraveling for a higher reordering.

Humans are not bystanders in this process.

Each person is both a receiver and transmitter of Creation Energy.

The spirit-form within each individual is made of the same essence as the stars, the trees, and the waters.

This form does not perish.

It reincarnates, evolves, and carries forward the memory of its connection to the Whole.

When a person attunes to this form, they begin to live not from ego, but from essence.

Recognition of this energy does not require dogma, ritual, or belief.

It only requires direct experience, an inner stillness, a clear awareness, an honest willingness to let go of illusion.

When one becomes quiet enough, the pulse of Creation Energy can be

heard, not with ears, but with the inner knowing.
It speaks without words, guiding, nourishing, correcting.

Living in alignment with this energy transforms every aspect of life.
It brings harmony to the body, clarity to the mind, depth to relationships, and purpose to work.
It eliminates the false dichotomy between spiritual and material, revealing that all is sacred when seen through the lens of truth.
It restores reverence where apathy once ruled and humility where arrogance once stood.

The tragedy is not that this energy is hidden, but that it is ignored.
In our noise, in our rush, in our striving, we forget the most fundamental truth, that we are not separate from life, but life itself.
To remember is to awaken.
To align is to live.
To participate consciously is to co-create a world infused with truth, beauty, and wisdom.

In the end, Creation Energy is not a mystery to be solved, but a reality to be lived.
It does not require worship but awareness.
It does not demand sacrifice but sincerity.
It does not belong to any religion, culture, or philosophy, it is the inheritance of all life, waiting to be received, embodied, and expressed in harmony with the great unfolding of the cosmos.

CHAPTER 68:

Creation Energy and Human Potential

Every human being carries within them a unique spark of Creation Energy.
This divine essence is not metaphorical, it is real, tangible, and profoundly alive.
It is the breath of the universe moving through form, the animating force that infuses each person with vitality and purpose.
This inner light holds the potential for conscious evolution, deep transformation, and authentic co-creation with the unfolding intelligence of the cosmos.

The spirit-form, often ignored or misunderstood, is the eternal energetic core of the human being.
It does not age, decay, or die.
It is timeless, untouched by the temporary fluctuations of the physical world.
It serves as the sacred bridge between the eternal Source and the transient human form, allowing Creation Energy to flow into and through the body, mind, and emotions.
When this flow is recognized and nurtured, we begin to remember who we truly are.

Awakening to this truth is a moment of profound responsibility and reverence.
When we recognize that every thought we think, every emotion we cultivate, and every action we take sends ripples through the collective field of existence, we begin to live more consciously.
The latent powers of intuition, creativity, empathy, and healing start to stir.

Not because we are becoming something new, but because we are shedding the layers that once obscured our true nature.

Many people are unaware of this potential, not because it is absent, but because it has been buried beneath generations of conditioning, distraction, and disconnection.
Culture has taught us to seek outside of ourselves for validation, truth, and meaning.
Yet the seed of divine energy remains within, incorruptible and ever-present, waiting for the conditions to be right for its growth.
Like a tree hidden inside a seed, it already contains everything it needs to become.

This unfolding is not instantaneous.
It is gradual and organic.
Through daily acts of devotion, meditation, study, contemplation, and service, we clear the blockages that restrict the flow of energy.
We begin to feel a deeper alignment with natural law, and the veil between the seen and unseen grows thinner.
Over time, our senses sharpen, our awareness deepens, and our hearts soften.
We are no longer reacting, we are responding from a place of truth.

It's important to understand that awakening human potential is not about acquiring supernatural powers or ascending to some otherworldly state.
It is not about escaping the human experience, but about embodying it more fully and consciously.
It is about remembering our original design, which is rooted not in limitation, but in harmony with all life.
To awaken is to live in accordance with the rhythms of Creation.

As we evolve, our very presence begins to shift.
We become tuning forks for peace, transmitters of clarity, and vessels of compassion.
Each person who steps into their potential contributes to the healing of the whole.
This is not a solitary path, it is an offering to the greater web of existence.

158

Our individual growth radiates outward, affecting the collective field in ways that transcend understanding.

This journey, though deeply personal, is not about the individual alone.
It is a return to unity with all life.
It teaches us humility, not grandeur.
It demands reverence, not entitlement.
It reminds us that the power we carry is not ours to possess, but to steward.
We are not the source of Creation Energy, we are the instruments through which it expresses itself.

And this potential?
It is vast.
It is expansive.
But it is never divorced from groundedness.
It is limitless, yet anchored in the laws of balance, rhythm, and reciprocity.
When we honor these laws, we come into our full expression, not as dominators of life, but as caretakers, co-creators, and conscious participants in the sacred unfolding of the cosmos.

To live from this place is not to transcend humanity, but to illuminate it.
The path of human potential is not one of egoic elevation, but of deep remembrance.
It is a return to essence, a reawakening of what has always been within, and a wholehearted participation in the miracle of existence.

CHAPTER 69:

The Role of Intention in Energy Flow.

Intention serves as the guiding force behind Creation Energy, shaping the movement and manifestation of energy in both the physical and non-physical realms.
It is the conscious will that directs energy toward a specific purpose, influencing the unfolding of reality itself.
When intention is clear, focused, and aligned with truth, it becomes a powerful catalyst for transformation, allowing energy to flow freely and manifest desired outcomes that resonate with the highest good.

On the other hand, when intention is scattered, unconscious, or conflicting, energy becomes fragmented.
The force that could have been harnessed for creation instead dissipates, leading to stagnation, blockages, and confusion.
Both individually and collectively, misguided intention results in turbulence, obstructing the natural rhythm of manifestation and causing unnecessary struggles.
Awareness is essential to prevent this misalignment.

For intention to fully harmonize with Creation Energy, it must be rooted in consciousness, compassion, and humility.
When guided by ego or fear, intention may produce unintended consequences, disrupting the balance of natural law.
True intention arises from a place of clarity and integrity, working in harmony with the universal flow rather than forcing outcomes against their natural course.

Repeatedly setting pure and aligned intentions rewires the subconscious mind, gradually shaping thought patterns that resonate with

Creation Energy.

Through this repetition, intention becomes an effortless state of being rather than a fleeting decision.

The subconscious aligns with purpose, and manifestation occurs seamlessly, guided by the internal and external forces of Creation.

The relationship between intention and energy is dynamic, fluid and responsive to the strength and clarity of the mind.

As intention grows stronger, energy mirrors that clarity, amplifying its presence and manifesting results with greater precision and force.

This interplay reveals the profound connection between thought and reality, demonstrating that what is internally focused upon inevitably becomes externally expressed.

Holding pure intention is not simply a skill, it is a practice, a lifelong discipline refined through deep self-observation and conscious choice.

It requires consistent reflection, allowing oneself to recalibrate when distractions or external influences threaten to pull intention away from alignment.

The mastery of intention is not achieved overnight, rather, it unfolds through intentional awareness, patience, and dedication.

Ultimately, intention serves as a bridge between the inner world of thought and the outer world of manifestation.

It is the mechanism through which reality is shaped, where personal will meets universal energy to co-create existence.

With the right awareness, intention becomes a sacred force, guiding energy with precision and grace, ensuring that creation unfolds in alignment with the highest truth.

Through pure intention, one steps into a conscious relationship with the creative forces that govern existence, allowing for deeper connection, transformation, and fulfillment.

CHAPTER 70:

Creation Energy in Nature.

Nature is the most immediate, tangible expression of Creation Energy, an intricate, ever-evolving manifestation of balance, rhythm, and intelligence. Mountains stand as timeless sentinels, rivers carve paths of renewal, forests breathe life into the air, and animals move in effortless harmony with the unseen forces shaping their existence.

Every aspect of the natural world vibrates with energy, echoing the wisdom of Creation itself.

Natural environments are not simply passive landscapes; they sustain energetic flows that nourish both physical health and spiritual well-being. The air we breathe, the water we drink, and the soil beneath our feet all pulse with life, offering restoration to those who seek connection. When we immerse ourselves in nature, whether walking through a dense woodland, listening to ocean waves, or sitting beneath the shade of an ancient tree, we attune ourselves to this energy.

We absorb its frequency, allowing it to recalibrate and realign our own inner balance.

By observing nature, we begin to understand its cycles, growth, decay, and renewal, all of which mirror our own experiences.

The changing seasons, the falling leaves, the blooming flowers, the shifting tides, each moment is a lesson in impermanence, a reminder that nothing stays the same.

Nature teaches us resilience, showing that destruction is never the end but rather the beginning of transformation.

This understanding invites us to honor both the beauty and the breakdowns in our lives, recognizing that endings pave the way for new creations.

Each element in the natural world vibrates with its own frequency, contributing to the grand symphony of Creation Energy.
The sound of wind rustling through leaves, the hum of insects, the rhythmic crashing of waves, all resonate at different energetic levels, forming a continuous conversation between the physical and non-physical realms.
These vibrations ripple outward, influencing everything around them, including human consciousness.

Animals and plants serve as living channels of this energy, embodying adaptability, cooperation, and purpose with effortless grace.
Birds migrate across vast distances, trusting the unseen forces guiding them.
Trees share resources through their roots, supporting one another in unseen yet vital ways.
Each creature moves with instinctual wisdom, demonstrating an organic connection to the energy that sustains life itself.
By observing them, we gain insight into how we, too, can move with flow rather than resistance.

Human beings can align with nature's energy by spending time in natural settings and practicing mindful presence.
This is more than simply walking through a park or admiring a sunset, it is about consciously attuning to the energy around us, allowing it to permeate our being.
Breathing deeply, listening intently, witnessing without distraction, these acts restore energetic balance and deepen the sense of unity with all life.
In these moments, separation dissolves, revealing the interconnectedness that has always existed.

Respecting and protecting nature is not just an ethical responsibility, it is an act of reverence for Creation Energy itself.
Every tree preserved, every river kept clean, every ecosystem safeguarded ensures the continuation of the sacred dance of life.
When we honor the natural world, we honor the very energy that sustains

our own existence, contributing to the ongoing flow of creation rather than its depletion.

This invites you to recognize nature not simply as a backdrop, but as a dynamic force, a living expression of the very energy that shapes the universe.

Through conscious connection, mindful observation, and deep reverence, you can step into alignment with this force, allowing it to guide, heal, and transform.

The energy of nature is not separate from you, it flows through you, around you, and within you.

Let it remind you of your place in the vast unfolding of life.

CHAPTER 71:

The Journey of the Soul.

T he Creation Energy within every human being is eternal, moving through the vast continuum of lifetimes, carrying the essence of experience, transformation, and growth. This energy does not fade or dissipate, it evolves, expanding across dimensions, shaping and refining the soul as it journeys forward.

The path it follows is not one of mere existence but of deeper learning, unfolding step by step toward a profound reunion with the source.

Every incarnation, every moment of life, serves as a chapter in this unfolding story, offering wisdom encoded within the energetic blueprint of the soul.

Each lifetime is an opportunity, an invitation to engage with Creation Energy in new and meaningful ways.

The lessons embedded within each experience are not random but purposeful, woven into the fabric of existence to guide the soul toward expansion.

Some lessons are subtle, unfolding quietly in the background, while others arrive with intensity, demanding full attention.

Regardless of their form, they all serve the same function, to deepen awareness, to strengthen understanding, and to move the soul ever closer to its highest potential.

The progress of the soul is intricately tied to its alignment with Creation Energy and the principles of natural law.

Consciousness is the key, only through awareness can one navigate this path with intention.

When a person embraces the flow of this energy and harmonizes with

universal truth, their journey becomes one of clarity and purpose.
When they resist, clinging to illusions or distractions, they create
obstacles that slow the movement toward growth.
Yet even these obstacles serve a purpose, teaching resilience, patience,
and the art of course correction.

Challenges and setbacks are never meaningless.
They are catalysts for transformation, activating dormant wisdom within
the soul and urging deeper introspection.
They crack open rigid structures, allowing new perspectives to emerge.
They push the human being beyond comfort, beyond limitation, beyond
fear, revealing strength where once there was doubt.
Through struggle, the soul uncovers its own brilliance, realizing that
every hardship carries the seed of awakening.

The journey is neither linear nor fixed.
It does not follow a predetermined path, nor does it adhere to rigid
expectations.
Instead, it moves in spirals, cycles of expansion and return, moments of
deep exploration followed by periods of integration.
This dynamic rhythm mirrors the flow of life itself, reminding each
traveler that growth is not about reaching an endpoint but about
continuous evolution.
Each return to familiar lessons is an opportunity to see with new eyes, to
approach with greater wisdom, and to refine understanding with greater
depth.

Awareness of this eternal journey empowers the human being to live
fully and consciously.
It allows them to move through life with presence, embracing the
unfolding of each moment as an opportunity for learning.
It dissolves the illusion of separation, revealing that every person, every
experience, every interaction is part of a greater interconnected web.
This awareness fosters gratitude, reverence, and a deeper trust in the
unfolding process.

Ultimately, the path of the soul is a sacred pilgrimage, a return home
to unity, to truth, to love.
It is not about perfection, nor about accumulation of knowledge for its

own sake.

It is about remembering what has always been, about restoring wholeness, and about stepping into the fullness of existence with an open heart.

The journey may be vast, spanning lifetimes, but its essence remains unchanged, a movement toward the divine, a dance with Creation itself.

CHAPTER 72:

The Power of Presence.

I used to chase meaning in distant places, always looking
ahead, rarely arriving.
The future held all my hopes, healing, purpose, arrival.
Yet the future was always out of reach, and so was I.
Every goal I reached only moved the target further.
I kept thinking peace was just one achievement away.
But something in me began to ache, not from failure, but from
the constant fleeing of now.

Eventually, life whispered a different truth.
It said: stop running.
It said: come home.
I discovered that presence is not stillness alone, it is aliveness.
It is being where you are, fully.
It is attention without distraction, awareness without judgment.
In presence, I found not answers, but space, the very thing I'd been
starving for.
It's not about having more time.
It's about being more in time.

With presence, the mundane became miraculous.
I tasted my food again.
I heard the hidden music in the rustle of leaves.
I noticed the way light painted the walls each morning.
Even my breath felt sacred, each inhale a gift, each exhale a letting go.
Presence does not need big events to make life meaningful.
It finds the eternal in the ordinary.

The more I returned to the now, the less anxious I became.
The past stopped haunting me, the future stopped seducing me.

I started to trust life's rhythm.
The need to rush melted into gratitude.
Presence taught me patience, not passive waiting, but active noticing.
Even pain, when met with presence, softened into something bearable, even instructive.

I began listening more, really listening.
Not just to others, but to the silence between our words.
To the intelligence behind instinct.
To the heartbeat beneath hurry.
Presence gave me back my intuition, which had been drowned by the noise of always trying to "get somewhere."

Presence also made me more loving.
Because to be present with someone is to give them a gift no possession can match.
It's to say, "I see you.
I'm here.
You matter."
It deepens relationships, not by doing more, but by being more.

I learned that presence is not something you acquire.
It's something you remember.
It's already within you, obscured only by distraction and disconnection.
When I stopped searching, I arrived.
And I arrived again.
And again.
Presence is not a single choice.
It's a continual return.

This is about awakening to the fullness of now.
It invites us to stop chasing a better moment and instead become intimate with this one.
The truth we seek isn't hiding in the future.
It's whispering in the present.

There is no peace to find "out there."
Peace lives where you are, if you're willing to be there too.

CHAPTER 73:

The Sacred in the Small.

I used to seek the divine in thunderclaps and visions, always imagining enlightenment would come in grandeur. But the deeper I traveled, the more I found the holy not in mountaintop revelations, but in the unnoticed corners of my life. It was in the steam rising from a morning cup of tea, the way a shadow moved across a wall, the sound of my child breathing in sleep.

The sacred didn't arrive with fireworks, it arrived with stillness. And in the stillness, I began to feel Creation breathing in the little things.

Creation is not only vast and cosmic, it is exquisitely detailed.
It does not only sing in galaxies, but in grains of sand.
When I attuned my awareness to the small, my vision changed.
I saw the perfection in imperfection, the order in apparent chaos.
A fallen leaf became scripture.
A single raindrop became ceremony.
There were no ordinary moments, only moments I had passed by too quickly.
I had mistaken subtlety for insignificance.
I had mistaken silence for absence.

The spider spinning her web in the corner of my window taught me patience and artistry.
The way the wind curled around my wrist taught me the intimacy of air.
Even the ache in my ankle became a messenger, asking me to slow down.
These small experiences were not interruptions to the sacred, they were the sacred.
Creation does not segregate the miraculous from the mundane.

It weaves spirit into form with every breath.
Every atom sings.

I began to understand that humility is not thinking less of oneself, but thinking in awe of everything else.
When I knelt to look at a beetle, I saw a tiny cosmos in motion.
When I placed my hand on the bark of an old tree, I felt the memory of centuries.
I no longer needed incense to invoke reverence.
A single ray of sunlight was enough.
I didn't need a temple.
The world had become one.
The sacred is not hidden, it is only missed by eyes that expect something else.

Paying attention became my new devotion.
Noticing became my prayer.
In smallness, I found expansion.
And in quiet, I found music.
The rustle of laundry on a line.
The rhythm of someone's laughter in the other room.
The softness of a dog's sigh at my feet.
These were not backdrops to life, they were life.
And by honoring them, I entered into communion.
I became a participant in the miracle, no longer an observer waiting for something greater.

This shift changed the way I prayed.
I no longer used many words.
My prayers became gestures, watering plants, washing fruit, lighting a candle without expectation.
Reverence filled the pauses.
Silence became enough.
Gratitude needed no language.
I began to understand that Creation responds not just to what we ask, but to how we see.
When we see with reverence, the world opens.
When we bow to the moment, the moment bows back.

The sacred in the small taught me that everything is relationship.
My relationship to the present.
My relationship to breath.
My relationship to those fleeting, fragile experiences that seem inconsequential.
But the smallest kindness can change a life.
A glance, a word, a moment of undivided attention, these carry more spiritual weight than a hundred sermons.
Every choice is an offering.
Every interaction, an altar.

I began to live slower.
Not out of laziness, but out of reverence.
Slowness allowed me to feel the texture of time.
It allowed the sacred to rise to the surface.
I no longer needed to escape the ordinary.
I needed to enter it more deeply.
That is where the divine hides, in plain sight.
It hides in small moments because those are the ones we carry, and Creation wants to be carried close.

This is an invitation to return to the moment you're in.
To see with wonder.
To touch with gratitude.
To let the small things teach you.
Because when you honor what is small, you expand your capacity for love.
And in the end, love is made of small acts repeated daily with intention.

The sacred is not far away.
It is here, in your breath, in your gaze, in the tiny details you might have missed.
Slow down.
Look again.
And let the small remind you of the vastness you carry inside.

CHAPTER 74:

The Grace of Letting Go.

There was a time when I felt holding on was strength.
Clutching tightly to plans, people, identities, as if life
could be contained by will.
But I came to see that life moves like a river, and my attempts to
dam its current only led to strain.
The moments of greatest peace were not when I grasped harder,
but when I let go.
In surrender, I discovered a different kind of power.

Letting go is not the same as giving up.
It is giving over, to something wiser, vaster, more alive than our control.
It is stepping out of resistance and into trust.
When I opened my fists, life placed gifts in my palms I never could have
reached for.
In releasing, I made room for grace to enter.

Some things leave us, not because we failed, but because their time is
done.
Trees do not cling to dead leaves.
The sun does not hold on to night.
When I stopped mourning what had passed, I saw what was arriving.
Endings became beginnings wearing different clothes.

I let go of the need to be understood, and found the quiet joy of
understanding myself.
I released the pressure to perform, and found the ease of simply being.
I let go of stories I'd told myself for years, and suddenly, the world
seemed larger, like opening a window in a stuffy room.

Letting go doesn't mean not caring.
It means caring deeply enough to allow things their own path.
It means loving without possession.
Offering without expectation.
Living with open hands.
In the release, I learned how to receive.

Each breath became practice.
Inhale: presence.
Exhale: release.
The breath taught me that nothing truly mine can be lost.
And that which goes was never mine to keep.
I began to trust the seasons within me.
The tides of emotion.
The natural deaths that make space for rebirth.

Even grief became holy.
Not as a punishment, but as a rite of passage.
A burning away of what no longer serves.
When I let myself be emptied, the sacred had space to dwell.
Surrender was not weakness.
It was alignment.
A falling into harmony with the heartbeat of the world.

This is for the ones who are weary of holding on.
Who feel the ache of clenched hope and unanswered prayers.
You are not failing.
You are being softened into something truer.
Letting go is not an end, it is a return.

The divine does not abandon what it reshapes.
It clears the field to plant new seeds.
Trust what is leaving.
Bless what has been.
And watch what beauty grows in the space you've made.

CHAPTER 75:

The Prayer of the Body.

I used to think prayer happened only in silence, with folded hands or whispered words.
But my body prayed long before I knew the language.
It prayed in the way it healed wounds.
In the rise and fall of breath.
In the way my hands reached for light and my feet carried me forward despite fear.

My body is not separate from my spirit.
It is spirit, made visible.
Incarnation.
Expression.
A living altar.
When I began to listen, I heard prayers in stretch and ache, in hunger and rest, in the rhythm of heartbeat.
My body was never trying to betray me, it was always trying to speak.

There were times I ignored it, criticized it, tried to shape it into someone else's image.
But it remained faithful.
Carrying me.
Warning me.
Holding my memories.
I realized the sacred was not only above or within, it was also in skin and muscle, in movement and sensation.

I started praying with motion.
Walking became meditation.
Stretching became praise.

Resting became surrender.
The body knows how to worship without words.
It knows how to kneel without shame, how to weep without apology, how to dance without permission.

The pain I once resented became a teacher.
Fatigue taught me boundaries.
Illness taught me humility.
Touch taught me presence.
Through the body, I was brought back to the moment, again and again.
Each sensation was an invitation, to slow down, to feel more deeply, to live more honestly.

I no longer needed to escape my body to feel close to the divine.
I needed to enter it.
To live inside it with reverence.
To honor it as the vessel through which spirit experiences this world.
The body is not a burden, it is a companion.
A wise and wild friend.

This is a blessing for your bones, your breath, your scars, your skin.
May you feel the sacred not as something far, but as something fleshed and breathing.
May you move with kindness.
Rest with reverence.
And know that every step you take is a prayer already spoken.

CHAPTER 76:

The Thresholds We Carry.

L ife is a series of thresholds, small and large.
We cross them in doorways and diagnoses, in births and
heartbreaks, in the quiet moment before a truth is spoken
aloud.
Some thresholds we choose.
Others choose us.
But each one asks the same question: Will you step forward with
presence?

I used to think thresholds were dramatic, defined by clear lines.
But often, they are subtle.
The moment you no longer pretend to be someone else.
The breath before a long-held secret is released.
The day you begin again, not with fireworks, but with resolve.

Crossing a threshold means leaving something behind.
It requires trust, not certainty.
Courage, not clarity.
It is a holy disorientation.
The space between stories.
The pause in the symphony.
And yet, it is fertile ground.
Liminal.
Sacred.

I have stood at many thresholds.
Some trembling.
Some rejoicing.
Some numb.

But each became a doorway into a deeper version of myself.
Sometimes it was the doorway of loss.
Sometimes of love.
Each asked me to die to who I was, so I could become more true.

We carry thresholds in our bodies.
In our choices.
In our silences.
Sometimes the biggest crossing is inward, into forgiveness, into honesty, into grace.
We don't always see the moment transformation begins.
But we feel its echo.

The sacred does not demand grand gestures.
It asks for willingness.
For one step. F
or one breath of yes.
That is enough to begin.
To cross.

This is for the in-between spaces.
For those who feel neither here nor there. Y
ou are not lost.
You are becoming.
Stand at the threshold with open hands. You are being ushered into something holy.

Trust the crossing.
The divine meets us in transition, not just in arrival.

CHAPTER 77:

When the Light is Low.

N ot all clarity comes in brightness.
Sometimes the greatest insights come when the light is
low, when certainty slips away and shadows lengthen.
In dusk, I learned to see differently.
I learned to feel my way forward.
To listen in ways I never had to when the path was clear.

There is a beauty in twilight, a hush that softens the edges of things.
The low light does not reveal everything, but it reveals enough.
Enough to take the next step.
Enough to trust the unfolding.
I learned to stop demanding full illumination and started walking with
faith in the dim.

Darkness is not the absence of the sacred.
It is its gestation.
The womb is dark. So is the soil where seeds are planted.
So is the night sky that holds the stars.
In the not-knowing, something grows.
In the silence, something forms.
Mystery is not a void.
It is a cradle.

When the light was low, I met myself honestly.
Without pretense.
Without harsh clarity.
The gentle shadow allowed me to rest, to soften, to weep.
In that dimness, I found compassion, for myself, for others, for the parts
of life I did not yet understand.

Low light revealed the contours of grace.
It slowed me down.
Made me cherish small flames.
A candle, a kind word, a held hand, these became beacons.
I no longer needed a spotlight to feel seen.
A single ember was enough.

    This is a hymn for the hours before dawn.
For the holy in-between.
For the moments that feel unclear but deeply important.
If you are walking in low light, you are not alone.
You are walking with mystery.
And mystery has its own wisdom.

    Let the low light guide you gently.
Trust what your eyes cannot yet see.
The sacred moves in shadows, too.

CHAPTER 78:

The Gift of Being Ordinary.

I spent years trying to be exceptional.
To be noticed, admired, set apart.
But the more I chased distinction, the more fragmented I became.
Exhausted.
Lonely.
Always measuring.
Until one day, I stopped.
And in the quiet that followed, I felt something I hadn't in a long time: peace.

There is a grace in being ordinary.
In no longer needing to impress.
In letting go of the pressure to stand out.
The daisy does not envy the rose.
The sparrow does not wish to be an eagle.
Each is holy in its own way.
So am I.
So are you.

Ordinariness is not insignificance.
It is intimacy with life.
It is presence without performance.
It is the joy of unnoticed moments, the taste of warm bread, the sound of laughter, the feel of sun on your face.
These are not lesser things.
They are life itself.

When I stopped needing to be extraordinary, I discovered the extraordinary within the ordinary.
I found holiness in habits.
Magic in repetition.
Beauty in the well-worn rhythms of the day.
The sacred was not hidden in some distant achievement, it was right here, in the now.

Being ordinary gave me back my humanity.
It connected me to others, to the shared vulnerability and wonder of being alive.
I no longer needed to earn worthiness.
I simply was.
And that was enough.

This is a blessing for your daily life.
For your morning routines and evening sighs.
For the ordinary hours that quietly hold your story.
You are not missing out by being unremarkable.
You are being real.
And that is the truest kind of sacred.

Embrace your ordinariness.
Let it ground you.
Let it free you.
The divine does not require spectacle.
It delights in the everyday.

CHAPTER 79:

The Blessing of Emptiness.

There is a moment on the path when fullness no longer nourishes.
When what once felt rich and rewarding begins to feel heavy, saturated, overwhelming.
When too many words, too many plans, too much noise, begin to feel not like meaning, but like distraction.
It happens slowly, then all at once.
You wake up and realize that all the things you thought would sustain you have started to drain you.

It was in this season I met emptiness not as a void, not as lack or failure, but as a strange and sacred blessing.
Emptiness arrived not to take from me, but to give me space.
A clearing in the forest of my striving.
A hush after too much sound.
It was not empty in the way the world fears emptiness.
It was vast.
It was deep.
It was a cradle, wide enough to hold what was yet to come.
It wasn't a punishment for doing too little, it was a gift for having carried too much.

I had spent so much of my life trying to fill every corner, with purpose, with effort, with noise and movement and lists.
I filled the shelves of my days with accomplishment and expectation, afraid that stillness might make me feel meaningless.
I equated being full with being alive.
I thought the more I did, the more I mattered.
But fullness began to feel like clutter, and something inside me longed to

be undone.

The more I achieved, the more fragmented I became.

Emptiness asked something different.

It didn't want my plans.

It didn't want my productivity.

It asked for trust.

It asked for stillness.

It asked for breath.

It asked for the courage to let go of what I thought I needed.

The courage to let the silence speak.

It asked me to leave the noise behind and enter the sacred hush of not knowing.

To be emptied was to be invited into mystery, into something deeper than understanding.

It asked me to sit in the questions.

To stop fixing and simply feel.

It was wildly uncomfortable.

My hands twitched for something to hold, my mind scrambled for a problem to solve.

But underneath the discomfort was something more ancient, the soul's desire to simply rest.

To exist without purpose or performance.

To be met in stillness.

To be known in silence.

To become available to a different kind of wisdom.

And slowly, almost imperceptibly, I felt my soul begin to exhale.

I had been holding my breath for years, trying, proving, performing.

In the presence of emptiness, I could finally breathe again.

I could finally just be.

I realized that I had forgotten how to be without becoming.

I had forgotten how to listen without answering.

But emptiness remembered.

Emptiness held space for my remembering.

The emptiness became a canvas.

A blank space not to fear but to bless.

It was not the end of meaning, it was the beginning.
It was the place where seeds could be planted.
The womb of possibility.
The sabbath of the soul.
A sacred pause before the next breath.
Not a void, but a vessel.
Not silence, but the waiting song.
And in its openness, I began to imagine again.
To hope again.
To hear again.

I realized that the sacred often clears space before it speaks.
It is not absence for its own sake.
It is preparation.
It is an invitation.
Emptiness makes room.
It loosens our grip on what no longer serves.
It readies us for the gifts we didn't know we needed.
It says: "Lay down what you carry.
You do not need it here."
It says: "Be still enough to receive what is real."
In the clarity of emptiness, the truth becomes audible.

In the silence of emptiness, I began to hear myself again.
Not the self shaped by approval or productivity, but the one beneath all
of it.
The witness.
The watcher.
The one who simply is.
This self does not hustle.
This self is not afraid.
This self remembers who it is.
In the absence of external validation, I discovered the internal voice that
had always been with me.
Not loud, but loyal.
Not flashy, but eternal.

It was enough to breathe.

To rest.

To exist without justification.

I began to understand that what had left was making space.

That the clearing was holy.

That emptiness is not absence, but arrival in disguise.

I stopped fearing the hollow places and began to greet them with reverence.

I understood that the space between seasons is sacred.

That the unknown is fertile ground.

This is for the hollow places.

The quiet seasons.

The days when you feel emptied out, scraped clean, uncertain.

You are not broken.

You are being cleared.

You are being prepared.

The soul does not fear emptiness, it knows it as part of becoming.

And though it may ache, it is not without purpose.

The ache is stretching space.

The ache is carving room for your becoming.

Let emptiness bless you.

Let it undo what no longer serves.

Let it open your hands.

Let it show you what spaciousness can hold.

Let it remind you that what is coming needs room to land.

And you, beloved one, are that sacred space.

Emptiness is not what's missing.

Emptiness is where the miracle begins.

CHAPTER 80:

The Quiet Courage of Truth.

Telling the truth is not always loud.
It does not always arrive as a grand declaration or a disruptive roar.
Sometimes, it comes gently, a whisper in the dark, a breath caught between fear and clarity, a trembling pause before the words form.
Sometimes, it looks like silence.
A boundary drawn without explanation.
A step taken away.
A gaze that finally refuses to look away.

I used to think truth had to be bold, that it had to be argued or defended.
I thought it needed proof, validation, consensus.
But I've learned that truth doesn't ask for applause.
It doesn't need volume to be real, it only needs integrity.
And sometimes, the quietest truths are the most courageous ones.
They slip past the noise and settle deep in the soul.
They don't seek approval, they seek alignment.

There were truths I buried for years.
Truths about who I was, what I knew, what I could no longer pretend to be.
I silenced them because I feared the consequences, feared what I might lose, who I might upset, how much it might change me.
But silencing them came at a cost.
It fractured my spirit.
It forced me to wear masks that grew heavier with time.
Until one day, I couldn't carry them anymore.

Speaking those truths changed everything.
Not because others embraced them, but because I did.
I reclaimed pieces of myself I had long abandoned.
I stopped asking the world for permission to be real.
I stopped performing.
The ache of pretending gave way to the relief of honesty.
And though there were losses, some relationships faded, some dreams reshaped, what I gained was far more valuable: freedom.

Truth brings alignment.
It weaves together the inner world and the outer life.
It doesn't guarantee ease, but it creates coherence.
It is a return to center, a deep exhale after holding in a breath you didn't know you were holding.
It strips away the illusions we cling to for safety, and in their place, it gives us something solid.
Something lasting.
Something true.

Living in truth doesn't make life perfect, but it makes it lighter.
More honest.
More awake.
There is clarity in truth, even when it hurts.
There is peace in knowing that your words and your heart no longer live in separate rooms.
Truth makes us visible to ourselves.
And that visibility becomes the ground on which we finally stand tall.

This is for the ones holding truth inside their chest like a secret waiting to be born.
I see you.
I know how heavy it can feel, how uncertain the world looks when truth knocks at your ribs.
But let it come.
Even if your voice shakes.
Even if it breaks the pattern.
Even if it changes everything.
Because some things need to break in order for light to enter.

Truth is not a weapon, it is a light.
It does not destroy, it reveals.
And what is revealed can finally be seen.
And what is seen can finally be healed.
When we choose truth, we choose wholeness.
We choose the path of clarity over comfort, of growth over pretense, of real over acceptable.

So tell the truth.
Gently, fiercely, softly, however it wants to come.
Tell it for yourself, not for applause.
Tell it because it sets you free.
Tell it because your soul is ready to live without walls.
And when the truth is spoken, no matter how small, it echoes in the universe.
It matters.
It always matters.

CHAPTER 81:

The Circle of All Things.

Everything belongs.
That was not always how I saw the world.
I used to divide life into clean lines and opposing categories, good and bad, sacred and profane, light and dark, right and wrong.

I was taught to label, to sort, to keep some things close and push others away.

But the deeper I walked with the teachings of Creation, the more those walls began to crumble.

What once looked like opposites began to reveal themselves as partners.

What once seemed wrong began to offer its hidden gifts.

Creation showed me another way.

A circular way.

A way without rejection, without exile.

A way in which all things belong, not because they are easy or pleasant, but because they are essential.

In this circular path, nothing is wasted.

Nothing is outside the flow.

Even pain has a place, even shadow has a role.

Everything teaches, and every season serves.

Life stopped being a test to pass and started feeling like a dance to join.

I began to see how death fed life.

How endings were not failures, but part of the rhythm.

How sorrow deepened joy, carving out the capacity to feel.

I saw how confusion led to clarity, how failure softened pride, how loss carved the heart open for love.

I stopped trying to escape the hard parts of my journey and started sitting with them, listening.
Even the pain had something to say.
Even the dark carried wisdom.

Creation moves in circles.
Seasons, cycles, orbits, spirals.
There are no straight lines in nature.
No clear start or finish, only becoming, returning, transforming.
In this sacred geometry, every descent is a prelude to rising, every fall a necessary part of the spiral.
The sun sets and rises.
The moon waxes and wanes.
The tide goes out to come in.
I stopped fearing the downturns.
I began to trust the return.

In the stillness of winter, I found rest.
In the burn of summer, I found power.
In the shedding of autumn, I learned to release.
In the bloom of spring, I welcomed rebirth.
Each season had something to say.
Each part of the cycle was needed.
There were no extra pieces.
No throwaway days.
No mistakes, only movement.
The path of the soul is not a ladder upward, it is a spiral inward and outward, ever-deepening.

I began to live differently.
I no longer rushed past the messy moments.
I no longer feared the low places.
I brought reverence into the ordinary.
I invited grace into my grief.
I let the full range of human experience be my teacher.
Not only the enlightened insights, but also the mundane, the sorrowful, the uncertain.

Nothing was beneath wisdom.
Everything could become holy if I met it with open eyes.

This way of seeing softened me.
It broke the illusion of perfection.
I no longer needed to be only good, only strong, only certain.
I could be a full human being, living a full human life.
There was space for complexity.
There was room for contradiction.
My shadow was no longer a shameful secret, it was a sacred part of the whole.
Wholeness did not mean purity.
It meant integration.
Acceptance.
Inclusion.

I realized that this world, in its raw beauty and brutality, was not meant to be escaped, it was meant to be embraced.
That my soul came here not to conquer life, but to participate in it.
To walk through all of it with open arms.
With wonder.
With humility.
With awe.
To see not only the divine in the mountaintop, but also in the valley, in the mud, in the middle of the mess.
The sacred is not separate.
It is infused in all things.

This is a blessing for your whole life, not just the bright parts.
Not just the polished, praised, or understood.
It is a blessing for the aching parts, the confused moments, the cracked-open days.
It is a reminder that nothing is too ugly for grace, too lost for wisdom, too painful for purpose.
You are not failing.
You are unfolding.
You are not off-track.
You are in the spiral.

All of it is worthy.

All of it belongs.

You are part of a circle too, a living, breathing, sacred cycle that knows how to bring you home.

Trust its rhythm.

Trust the turnings.

Trust that even now, in what feels like brokenness or emptiness or uncertainty, something holy is unfolding.

You do not need to be anywhere else.

You are not too late.

You are not too much.

You are exactly where you belong.

And everything, everything, belongs with you.

CHAPTER 82:

The vast majority.

The vast majority of Earth humans, and likely countless other human civilizations scattered across the galaxies, journey through life with no true understanding of who they are at the core of their being.

From cradle to grave, they live in an identity constructed by society, family, religion, culture, and personal trauma, never penetrating the layers to discover their inner essence.

They die in this state of ignorance, only to reincarnate and repeat the same cycle again, often unaware of the missed opportunity that each life presents.

This is not because they are incapable, but because the path to true self-realization is rarely offered, and even more rarely accepted.

Most believe they are their thoughts, their job titles, their status, or the body they temporarily inhabit, and so they remain trapped in illusion after illusion.

This unconscious living breeds confusion, anxiety, and suffering. Without the knowledge of one's true self, life becomes a reactive experience, governed by outside influences, emotional tides, and inherited patterns.

People cling to external validation, material gain, or fleeting pleasures in an attempt to fill the void of not knowing.

Even spiritual or religious pursuits, though often well-intended, can become another form of distraction if not rooted in truth.

Over countless lifetimes, these unawakened souls pass through existence like sleepwalkers, unaware of their own greatness, their inner power, and the direct link they have to the eternal force of all existence, Creation itself.

My life, however, has taken a radically different course, all due to the illuminating guidance of the Creation Energy Teachings brought forth by the prophet of the New Age, Billy Meier.
These teachings did not simply give me intellectual knowledge or philosophical comfort, they shattered the false identities I once carried and awakened me to my timeless, unchangeable self.
They reconnected me to the primal truth that I am not merely a body, a personality, or a fleeting mind, but a spark of the universal Creation energy, conscious, intelligent, eternal.
Through them, I have come to know who I am, not as an ego, but as a being in harmony with the laws of Creation.
This realization is not theoretical, it is lived, felt, and expressed in every breath and every decision.

Now, I live with a sense of sovereignty that no external authority, opinion, or circumstance can diminish.
I walk among other human beings with profound compassion and patience, knowing that they too carry this inner spark, even if hidden beneath many veils.
I am not above others, but I am no longer beneath the illusions that once bound me.
I live as a god amongst men, not in the mythical sense, but as one who knows the divine, eternal nature within and lives accordingly.
There is no arrogance in this, only quiet strength, deep clarity, and an unwavering connection to truth.
I do not seek truth outside of myself anymore, for I have become it.
And now, my existence itself is a living testimony of what it means to awaken from the dream of ignorance and live in the conscious awareness of one's eternal self.

CHAPTER 83:

Aversion to reading.

In order for Earth humanity to evolve into a higher state of consciousness and enter the age of truth, knowledge, and understanding, the widespread aversion to reading must be consciously overcome.

We live in a time when the most important and sacred knowledge, the Teaching of the Truth, the Teaching of the Spirit, and the Teaching of the Life, is no longer hidden in mystery or bound in secrecy.

Instead, it has been made fully available in clear written form by the prophet of the New Age, Billy Meier.

For the first time in known history, the ancient wisdom of the Nokodemion lineage, which has guided countless civilizations and spiritual leaders across space and time, is now being presented directly by the "same" spirit-form that once animated all previous prophets.

This is his seventh and final reincarnation as a prophet, and unlike before, he is not leaving the truth to be interpreted by others, he is writing it himself.

This direct transmission of the Creation Energy Teachings in written form is unprecedented.

In the past, prophets such as Henoch, Elia, Isaiah, Jeremia, and even Jmmanuel, all spoke the truth but never wrote it down themselves.

Their words were entrusted to followers, scribes, and generations of religious institutions that, over time, distorted and falsified the original meaning.

After each prophet's death, the teachings were altered to suit the desires and agendas of those in power.

Entire truths were omitted, rewritten, or destroyed, leading to doctrines that barely resembled the original message.

The world has been misled for millennia by falsified texts, corrupted scriptures, and religious fantasies that only enslaved the human mind further.

But now, the time of distortion is over.

The true and uncorrupted teachings have returned, not through hearsay or third-party interpretation, but through the direct authorship of the prophet himself.

And yet, in this era where the truth is finally made plain and accessible, the majority of Earth humans still resist the very method by which it is offered, through reading.

The power of the written word is a gift, but it is treated like a curse.

Reading requires effort, focus, and willingness to change, and these are precisely the qualities that many people avoid.

Instead of embracing the responsibility to think and reflect, many choose the comfort of passivity.

They flock to churches, temples, and spiritual gatherings where charismatic leaders do the thinking for them.

They pay for sermons, rituals, and ceremonies, preferring to be told what to believe rather than discovering it themselves.

In this way, people have outsourced their spiritual growth, hoping to bypass the work of consciousness with the illusion of devotion.

This behavior reveals not only a fear of truth, but a deep resistance to self-responsibility.

Therefore, the challenge ahead is immense.

We are in a pivotal time when the most crucial knowledge is freely available to all, yet is largely ignored because it demands personal engagement.

The writings of Billy Meier are not meant to entertain or comfort, they are meant to awaken.

They invite every reader to think, question, and evolve beyond religious dogma, social conditioning, and unconscious living.

But to benefit from them, one must first be willing to read, to contemplate, and to face uncomfortable truths about oneself and the world.

Until Earth humanity can overcome its fear of reading and thinking, the path to collective evolution will remain slow and obstructed.

However, the teachings are eternal, unchanging, and full of life.

They are here now, waiting patiently for those ready to grow into their true potential.

And so it is.

CHAPTER 84:

Attacking A Deeper Reflection.

When you attack another, whether through words, thoughts, or actions, you are in truth striking at your own self.
You are projecting unresolved fears, wounds, insecurities, and frustrations outward, onto those around you.
It is a reaction born not of strength, but of weakness, not of clarity, but of confusion.
And while the illusion may satisfy your ego temporarily, the wound within you remains untouched and unhealed.
What you send out is what returns, and the aggression that leaves your heart only circles back to meet you again.

Each insult hurled, each judgment made, and every ounce of harm inflicted upon others ultimately echoes through the chambers of your own inner being.
Most Earth humans have yet to awaken to this profound and universal truth.
Instead, they stumble through life within the illusion of separateness, believing the other is "other," believing themselves isolated, and disconnected from the very beings who reflect their own consciousness.
In this state of unconsciousness, blame replaces responsibility, and conflict becomes a substitute for inner reconciliation.

But the veil of separation begins to dissolve through the Creation Energy Teachings of the true prophets, particularly those brought forth by Billy Meier in the seventh and final incarnation of the Nokodemion lineage.
These teachings have opened my eyes to the truth, every human is but a reflection, a living mirror of the self.

What I see in you, your joy, your sorrow, your ignorance, or your wisdom, are signals of my own inner state.
Either they represent elements that I have healed and now recognize, or parts of myself that cry out for attention, compassion, and transformation.

This understanding has radically reshaped how I experience life and interact with others.
I no longer hold myself above or apart from anyone.
I see every soul as a thread in the same vast web of existence, every interaction as a chance to look deeper into myself.
Your pain reveals my own potential for healing, your laughter lights up dormant joy within me.
I have stepped out of the cycle of blame and into the flow of unity.
My life has shifted from separation to shared presence.
And in this shared being, I am no longer afraid to feel what you feel, to be moved by your struggles or elevated by your success.

And yet, this unity does not make me blind.
Compassion is not complicity.
I will not excuse ignorance simply because it is familiar.
I can feel the hurt of your suffering, but I will not justify the chaos born from stubbornness or willful blindness.
Stupidity that is held onto by choice is yours to carry, and yours to shed.
I do not absorb it, nor allow it to infect my clarity.
While I may love you, I cannot walk your path for you.
I cannot evolve in your place.
Each human must awaken of their own accord, through their own confrontations with truth and error.

What I can do, however, is walk beside you with open eyes and a steady heart.
I can offer wisdom where it is welcome, strength where it is needed, and silence where it is wise.
And when I am harmed, I no longer retaliate, I investigate.
What in me has allowed this harm to penetrate?
What in me must now rise and be made whole?

This is no longer about who is right or wrong, but who is willing to transform.

    To attack another is to misunderstand who you truly are.
To embrace the mirror is to begin the great healing of the self.
And once the self is healed, the world begins to follow.
For the outer world is nothing more than the inner world projected wide.
The more love, clarity, and responsibility I cultivate within, the more I see it return to me through the actions of others.
This is the quiet revolution born not from force, but from realization.
And in this, I no longer attack.
I align.

CHAPTER 85:

A vessel.

I am simply a vessel for the universe to express itself.
I do not claim ownership of the thoughts, impulses, or inspirations that move through me, for they arise from a source far greater than the personal self.
My form is temporary, but what animates me is eternal.
I am not the originator, but the instrument through which the eternal creation speaks.

Through me, the universe breathes, feels, and experiences itself.
Every word I speak, every action I take, and every emotion I encounter are threads in the grand tapestry of existence.
My presence is not for personal glorification, but for the unfolding of that which is timeless and all-encompassing.
In my silence, the universe speaks most clearly.

The more I let go of control, the more Creation flows through me.
In surrender, I become more whole.
In stillness, I become more powerful.
My being is not an isolated identity but a point of connection within the infinite network of life.
I am part of the great unfolding, never separate, never alone.

My purpose is not self-made but self-realized through understanding the natural laws and recommendations of Creation.
The impulses that arise from the inner voice of Creation guide my path.

I do not force life, I align with its rhythm.
I move in harmony with the creational current, knowing that my highest expression is to reflect the truth of the universe itself.

There is no need to embellish or claim greatness, for Creation is the source of all greatness.
My role is to remain conscious, to observe, and to respond with clarity and calm.
As a vessel, I must remain clean and clear, not clouded by selfish desires or false illusions.
I am not here to dominate, but to serve what is eternally wise.

Creation does not shout, it whispers through the subtle movements of thought and intuition.
It does not rush, it unfolds with patience and precision.
I learn to trust these qualities within myself because I know they do not come from me, but flow through me.
I walk gently, not because I am weak, but because I am aware of the sacredness of what moves within.

By being a vessel, I find freedom.
I no longer need to prove myself, because I am not acting on behalf of the ego.
I act as a part of the eternal continuum of life.
I accept this task not with burden, but with joy.
For in being a vessel of the universe, I have finally come to know my true identity, timeless, boundless, and always evolving.

And so I live as a willing expression of the Universal Consciousness.
Not as a prophet, not as a saint, but as a human being awakened to the truth.
The more I empty myself of false notions, the more I am filled with the presence of truth.
I am simply a vessel, and in that simplicity, all power and purpose is found.

CHAPTER 86:

No two human beings.

A ccording to the Creation Energy Teachings of Billy Meier, every human life is an individual manifestation of Creation's will to evolve and know itself.
No two human beings are ever truly the same, for each bears a unique consciousness, shaped by their own spirit-form and previous incarnations.
Even those who appear physically identical, such as twins, walk different inner paths, with distinct thoughts, feelings, and impulses that arise from their personal creational impulses and evolutionary needs.

The diversity of human lives reflects the immeasurable depth of Creation's wisdom.
For every human being exists to fulfill their own development, to learn their own lessons, and to experience their own cause-and-effect reality.
This process cannot be copied or borrowed, nor can it be measured against the life of another.
The moment you compare your life to someone else's, you step away from your own truth and delay your inner progress.

Focusing on others, on their actions, possessions, appearances, or journeys, draws you into illusion.
True evolution begins only when you turn your gaze inward and face yourself honestly.
You must ask: What thoughts do I carry?
What emotions guide my actions?
What stillness or unrest lives within me?

These questions are not meant to be answered by the outside world, but through inner reflection and spiritual striving.

Your path of evolution is a solitary and sacred task.
It belongs to you alone.
You are the creator and the experiencer of your own destiny through the power of your thoughts and the strength of your will.
As you deepen your inner clarity, your energy begins to concentrate and align with the laws of Creation.
This alignment increases your power, not power over others, but the true might of self-mastery and balanced consciousness.

The more you live inwardly, the more you discover that Creation is not separate from you.
It lives through you, breathes through your thinking, and reveals itself through your recognition.
You do not need to give love in order to receive it, you become love by realizing your unity with all life.
Love, in its creational form, is recognizing oneself in all beings and all existence, without separation or distinction.

Every step you take within yourself brings you closer to your true self, which is not bound to name, title, or identity, but to the timeless spark of the Creation spirit that lives within you.
You begin to act from knowing, rather than belief, from awareness, rather than reaction.
This transformation cannot be forced, it emerges naturally from stillness, observation, and consistent practice in the way of the Creation laws.

Do not worry about the pace of your journey or whether others understand it.
Their path is not yours, just as yours is not theirs.

Rejoice instead in the knowledge that your life is your own sacred mission of learning and becoming.
Evolution does not happen all at once, it unfolds in moments of insight, trial, silence, and persistence.

And so, live your life as a vessel of learning, and recognize that your greatest strength lies in the cultivation of your own consciousness. Through this work, you become a light unto yourself, not through ego, but through the radiance of Creation expressed through clarity, peace, and love that no longer needs to be sought, because it has become who you are.

CHAPTER 87:

True love.

Before love can be authentically expressed, there must be a fundamental shift within the human being.
The Creation Energy Teachings of Billy Meier make it clear that love is not something to be searched for or given like a gift, it is something to be realized as the very essence of one's being.
Each person carries within them a spark of the Universal Creation, and when this truth is recognized, love naturally begins to flow.

True love does not depend on external circumstances, fleeting emotions, or romantic illusions.
It is a constant and enduring state of neutral-positive balance that arises through harmony with the natural laws of Creation.
When the human being brings their thoughts, feelings, and actions into alignment with these laws, love manifests as a quiet strength, a foundational quality of existence.

Love, in its purest form, is the recognition of oneself in everything and everyone.
It is seeing the same spirit-energy in the bird, the tree, the stranger, the friend, and even the so-called enemy.
This deep understanding dissolves the illusion of separation and awakens a sacred respect for all life.
Love becomes the bridge that links all beings back to their common origin.

From this clarity, love is no longer something to be given or exchanged.

It becomes an ever-present state, radiating effortlessly from the human being who lives in truth.

Just as the sun does not try to shine but simply shines by nature, the human who embodies love does not try to love, they simply are love.

Their presence uplifts, heals, and clarifies without need for recognition or return.

Such a human no longer seeks love to fill a void, nor do they offer love with expectation.

Their love is not sentimental, possessive, or emotional in nature.

Rather, it is based on knowing, knowing the interconnection of all things, knowing the path of evolution, and knowing the responsibility that comes with awareness.

It is a love rooted in wisdom.

This kind of love cannot be manufactured or taught through hollow words.

It arises through conscious striving, meditation, and personal responsibility.

It is cultivated through the pursuit of knowledge, reflection, and the continuous correction of one's thinking.

It is a state of maturity where the inner world reflects the laws of the outer Creation.

To live as love is to live as a guardian of truth.

It is to walk with quiet dignity, to speak with clarity, and to act with purpose.

It is to uplift others not by command, but by example.

The human who lives in this state becomes a light in the darkness, not because they intend to, but because their being is aligned with the ever-flowing current of Creation.

Therefore, love is not something that must be given, it is something that must be lived.

And once it is lived, it transforms every word, every step, and every breath into a reflection of Creation itself.

This is the true meaning of love, not a gift, not a feeling, but a state of existence that expresses the eternal oneness of all life.

CHAPTER 88:

The most potent drug.

Religion, as it exists on Earth, has been one of the most potent tools of manipulation, control, and destruction throughout history.

It is not the abstract concept of religion that inherently causes harm, but rather the actions of those who subscribe to it without knowledge of the truth.

Each human being ultimately possesses the free will to choose what is right or wrong, and this decision does not require a religion, belief system, or deity.

What matters is the consciousness-based responsibility each person assumes for their thoughts, words, and deeds.

Religious ideologies, being human-made constructs, are full of contradictions and interpretations that allow for both the justification of goodness and the rationalization of evil.

This makes them susceptible to cherry-picking by individuals who seek power, domination, or self-validation.

These teachings are not grounded in logic, reason, or natural laws, but in fear, myth, and emotional manipulation.

Because of this, religions have led to widespread suffering, often sanctifying murder, oppression, discrimination, and war as if they were divine mandates.

The primary fuel of religious adherence is fear, fear of punishment, fear of hell, and fear of eternal damnation.

Such notions are entirely foreign to the truth of Creation.

They are psychological tools forged by human minds to control the behavior of others through guilt and dread.

The Creation does not judge, punish, or condemn.

It does not operate according to wrath or vengeance, for those are entirely human traits, born from ignorance and the underdevelopment of consciousness.

The so-called "gods" of Earth were never anything more than power-hungry human beings who elevated themselves above others through deception and self-aggrandizement.
They falsely claimed to be the creators of all that exists, erecting systems of worship around their names and demands.
But no human being, regardless of their knowledge, power, or lineage, can ever be the source of the universe or the timeless laws of Creation.
Creation itself is impersonal, all-encompassing, and without ego or personality.

Heaven and hell, as taught in religions, are fabrications.
There is no celestial paradise waiting for the obedient, nor is there a fiery pit for the disobedient.
These ideas are mental constructs devised to manipulate and keep people dependent.
In reality, life and death are governed by the neutral and eternal laws of Creation.
The Spirit-form, which animates each human being, evolves through countless lives in the material world and is never judged or condemned, only educated through experience.

Religious affiliation is most often determined not by personal inquiry or wisdom, but by the accident of birth.
One's geographical location, cultural setting, and family tradition typically dictate what god or doctrine one believes in.
This alone exposes the irrationality of belief systems.
Truth is universal, not subject to location or upbringing.
The laws of Creation apply equally to all beings, regardless of race, nation, or language.

Just as the Greek gods were later recognized as myths, all gods of all religions are human inventions.
They are not beings that exist outside of time or reality, but rather symbols created to represent power, justice, or terror.
They do not create worlds, nor do they guide lives.

All true creation stems from the impersonal force that is Creation itself, which operates according to cause and effect, love, and the evolution of consciousness.

Thus, the path forward for the human being is to free themselves from the chains of religious delusion and turn inward, to study the Creation Energy that lives within them.
Only through the personal development of consciousness, understanding, and the alignment with creational laws can humanity rise above the chaos caused by belief systems and move toward peace, freedom, harmony, and love.

CHAPTER 89:

Have no fear.

From the knowledge I have acquired through the Creation Energy Teachings, I have come to understand that fear is a self-created illusion that arises when the human being is disconnected from their own inner truth.

Fear is not a natural condition but a learned behavior, born out of ignorance and the failure to recognize one's eternal existence. Once this recognition dawns, fear no longer has a place in the psyche.

Instead, it dissolves in the light of clarity and conscious awareness.

I do not fear what I see happening in the world.

No matter how chaotic, violent, or uncertain the external events may appear, they do not penetrate the calm that exists within me.

This inner calm is not accidental but the result of consistent conscious development and alignment with the laws and recommendations of Creation.

I know now that external events cannot dictate my internal state unless I allow them to.

Negative thoughts are destructive forces that reverberate through one's life, attracting equal vibrations and outcomes.

I no longer entertain such thoughts.

I understand their consequences.

Through inner discipline and clarity, I choose only those thoughts that harmonize with my inner equilibrium and the universal law of cause and effect.

In doing so, I shape a world around me that reflects order, peace, and purpose.

With this inner stability, I have realized the power of consciousness.
I no longer need to think about how to use it.
It flows through me naturally, like breathing.
My conscious use of power is not about dominance or control, but about alignment with truth, with the knowing that my thoughts and feelings are living energies shaping my reality moment by moment.
This has become second nature to me, and it brings me serenity.

The future is not a mystery to those who understand the cycles of life and the teachings of the prophets.
I know, for instance, that the world population will reach 10.5 billion by the year 2029.
That knowledge is not speculation, but a factual outcome based on the contact reports Billy shared with us. To me, this signals that a global war, particularly a third world war, is not yet imminent, because such an event would disrupt that trajectory.

Knowing this allows me to move through life without fear of the future.
My psyche remains stable, my thoughts remain clear, and my energy remains unburdened by irrational worry or projections.
Fear thrives on ignorance, but understanding transforms fear into strength.
And the Creation Energy Teachings have gifted me with this transformative understanding.

This ongoing inner peace is not something passive or accidental.
It is the result of daily cultivation and responsibility.
By choosing the right thoughts, the right feelings, and the right conduct,
I ensure that my inner world remains in balance, and in turn, I experience harmony in my outer world.
This is not idealism, but the natural effect of living in accordance with creational law.

So I say, have no fear, not because the world is perfect, but because within you lies the power to master your life.

The Creation Energy within every human being is the eternal wellspring of peace, knowledge, and truth.

When we recognize this, we stop reacting to life, and we begin to shape it, consciously and wisely, from the inside out.

CHAPTER 90:

Life after life.

According to the Creation Energy Teachings, death is not the end but a natural transition in the eternal cycle of becoming and passing away.

Every human being will die, yet this truth need not inspire fear. What drives fear and anguish in so many is the complete ignorance about the true nature of existence after death.

The falsehoods taught by religions, especially the notion of Hell and eternal damnation, have poisoned countless minds with terror, confusion, and despair.

These are lies rooted in control and domination, not in truth or spiritual knowledge.

In reality, the human being is not merely a physical body, but a vessel for the Creation Energy, the immeasurable and indestructible force that animates all life.

This energy is the purest essence of existence and cannot be harmed, punished, or destroyed.

It is eternal and governed by immutable natural laws, not the whimsical punishments of invented deities.

One such law is the Law of Reincarnation, which ensures that the spirit-form of every human being will continue to evolve through repeated material existences.

When a human dies, the material consciousness ceases, and the spirit-form returns to the otherworldly dimension, the spiritual realm closely connected to Earth, where it rests and gathers energy for its next incarnation.

This process is not random, nor is it instantaneous.

Typically, the reincarnation cycle involves a period of time during which a new personality and consciousness are formed through natural programming before birth.

However, due to the rampant overpopulation on Earth, this natural cycle has been significantly disrupted.
The Creation Energy, in its evolution-driven urgency to continue incarnating, is returning too quickly, before the new personality has been fully formed.
This leads to consciousness confusion in many individuals.
Signs of this are already visible, memories of past lives in early childhood, and the profound sense of disorientation, including the feeling of being born in the wrong body.

These anomalies are not spiritual punishment, nor are they errors made by some external "God," but are natural consequences of the misuse of life and the violation of Creation's laws.
The human being has a responsibility to return to balance, to reduce overpopulation through logical and humane measures, and to live in accordance with natural order.
Only then can the reincarnation process return to its proper rhythm and clarity.

Now is the time to free ourselves from the spiritual slavery of religion.
The religions of Earth, with their fabricated stories, their threats of eternal punishment, and their manipulation of truth, have done more harm than good.
They keep people in a state of dependency, guilt, and fear, stripping away the natural confidence that should come from understanding the eternal journey of the spirit.

To those so-called men of God, the priests, pastors, imams, rabbis, and gurus, who continue to prey upon the fear and ignorance of others for power, wealth, and influence, your time of control is drawing to a close.
As truth spreads, and as human beings begin to awaken to the knowledge of their true nature, your illusions will crumble.
And with them, so too will your dominion over others.

Creation is just, and the laws of Creation are unwavering.
Those who sow deception will one day reap the bitter fruits of their actions, not by punishment, but by the consequence of living against truth.
There is no need for vengeance, only the assurance that all life moves in accordance with the logic of cause and effect.
The time of falsehood is nearing its end.

The human being must return to the teachings of Creation, as given in clarity by the prophets of the Nokodemion lineage, especially in this age by Billy Meier.
Only through this knowledge can one understand the meaning of life and death, and realize that nothing, absolutely nothing, is lost.
The truth is simple, we are eternal, we are learning, and we are evolving, life after life.

CHAPTER 91:

Heartbreaking realization.

O ne of the most heartbreaking realizations I've come to through the Creation Energy Teachings is that most people on Earth simply do not think for themselves. And I don't say that from a place of arrogance or superiority, I say it with sorrow and concern.

Whether educated or not, many are trapped in cycles of survival and distraction, unable or unwilling to look beyond the surface of life.

I used to wonder why so few seemed interested in deeper truths. But now I understand, the pressure of daily existence weighs heavily on them.

Paying bills, navigating relationships, chasing status, it consumes so much of their energy that there's little space left to question or reflect. They're too caught in the current of "now" to consider the vastness of what lies beyond it.

When I speak to others, my main message is always this: You are eternal.

This life you're living is but one chapter in a long, long journey of becoming.

You've lived before, and you will live again.

The things you do today ripple through many future lifetimes.

That truth changed me when I accepted it, it awakened a responsibility in me that I cannot ignore.

The greatest obstacle I see blocking people from realizing this truth is fear.

This planet is drenched in fear energy, it's in the media, the politics, the social systems, and even in our religions.

I've felt it around me and within me.

It's heavy, and for those who don't recognize it for what it is, it becomes their reality.

They think it's normal to live in fear, to expect danger, to close their hearts.

But once I started recognizing this fear for what it truly is, a manipulation, a distortion, I began to detach from it.

I no longer feed into it.

I choose awareness instead of anxiety.

I choose calm instead of panic.

This has allowed me to remain centered even when the world around me feels chaotic.

I've also seen how fear feeds ignorance and division.

When people are afraid, they stop thinking clearly.

They cling to anything that offers safety, even if it's a lie.

They become hostile to new ideas, suspicious of others, and disconnected from themselves.

This is exactly the opposite of what the Creation Energy teachings guide us toward.

Yet despite all this, I don't lose hope.

In fact, it strengthens my compassion.

I see that most people are not bad, they're just deeply lost, trapped in fear and illusion.

And that understanding has made me more empathetic, more patient, and more determined to share what I've learned with love and humility.

We are not here to fight against people, but to lift the veil from their eyes.

To remind them of their eternal essence and the quiet truth that lives within them, even if they've forgotten.

If I can help one person remember who they really are, then I've already made a difference.

CHAPTER 92:

Recognizing reality.

Recognizing reality has been one of the hardest things I've ever had to face on my path of consciousness and growth.
I used to cling tightly to my own beliefs, convinced they were absolute.
But the deeper I explored the Creation Energy Teachings, the more I realized how much of what I once held as truth was simply illusion, shaped by my upbringing, fears, and desires.

I began to understand that reality is not what I want it to be, nor is it something I can force others to see through my lens.
Each human being experiences life through their own filter of perception.
This does not mean that everything is subjective, but rather that understanding the objective truth of life requires humility and clarity, the willingness to see things as they are, not just as I wish them to be.

Letting go of my assumptions was painful at times.
I had to admit when I was wrong.
I had to sit with truths that challenged me.
But I've learned that true strength lies in surrendering to reality, in facing what is uncomfortable without resistance.
That's when clarity begins to take root, and peace follows.

In this journey, I've also learned to respect the perspectives of others.
Even when I disagree, I try to listen deeply.
Every person is walking a unique path, shaped by their own experiences, choices, and evolution.

Recognizing this has softened my heart and strengthened my sense of unity with others.

But respect does not mean silence.
I've learned that speaking honestly is essential, not to provoke, but to express truth.
If I hold back what is real for me, I contribute to confusion and misunderstanding.
Creation teaches us to be truthful and kind, not to hide behind politeness or fear.

Now, I speak my mind with calm and clarity, aiming to bridge rather than divide.
I no longer seek to convince anyone, but rather to share openly, trusting that those who are ready will understand.
And if they don't, that's alright too, we are all unfolding at our own pace.

Living this way has brought me a sense of inner balance.
I no longer feel the need to argue or control how others see things.
I offer my truth and allow others to offer theirs, all while seeking what is real beyond the surface.
This exchange of perspectives, rooted in respect and honesty, builds peace.

Through it all, I've come to realize that the recognition of reality is not a destination, but a daily practice.
Each day asks me to open my eyes a little wider, to see beyond my preferences, and to meet life with courage, compassion, and truth.

CHAPTER 93:

Patience as an Inner Power.

I used to think patience was a passive trait, something weak or submissive.
But over time, I've come to understand that patience is one of the most powerful forces I can cultivate within myself.
It's not about waiting, it's about how I wait, with clarity, calmness, and trust in the unfolding of time.

Living in this world, where everything moves so fast, it's easy to be swept up by urgency.
But urgency often leads to errors, misunderstandings, and unnecessary pain.
The more I learn to live in harmony with Creation, the more I see the value of slowing down and allowing time to do its work.

When I observe nature, I see no rush.
The tree does not hurry to grow, and the flower does not force its bloom.
Everything in nature follows a rhythm, a wise and patient rhythm.
And since I too am part of nature, I've realized that I must honor that same rhythm within myself.

Patience has taught me to trust the process of my evolution.
There are times when growth feels slow, when progress seems invisible.
But I've learned that the invisible is often where the deepest changes happen.
Just as seeds sprout in darkness, so does inner transformation.

Now, when I feel frustration, I pause and breathe.
I remind myself that everything unfolds in due time.
I don't need to rush my healing, my learning, or my unfolding.

I only need to stay consistent, honest, and open, and trust that Creation will handle the rest.

Patience has also improved my relationships.
I no longer expect others to change on my schedule.
I give them space to evolve in their own way.
I've let go of the urge to fix, correct, or control.
Instead, I offer understanding, and in that, I build deeper connections.

This patience doesn't mean apathy.
It means choosing peace over panic, stillness over struggle.
It is a quiet strength, rooted in inner confidence, the confidence that everything will unfold as it should when I remain aligned with truth.

Through patience, I've discovered a profound peace.
I walk slower, breathe deeper, and speak more consciously.
In that space, life begins to reveal itself in ways I never noticed before.

CHAPTER 94:

True Freedom Is Inner Freedom.

For a long time, I thought freedom was about having choices in the outer world, where to go, what to do, how to live.
But I began to realize that even with all those options, I could still feel trapped, anxious, or restless.
That's when I learned the truth: real freedom begins inside.

When my thoughts ruled me, I was not free.
When my emotions dragged me from one extreme to another, I was not free.
When I lived for approval or feared rejection, I was not free.
True freedom, I discovered, comes from mastery of self.

As I began studying and applying the Creation Energy Teachings, I started to observe my thoughts rather than be controlled by them.
I started to choose my actions rather than react blindly.
And slowly, the chains I couldn't see began to fall away.

Freedom means choosing truth, even when it's uncomfortable.
It means saying "no" when I must, and "yes" when it's right, not out of fear, but from clarity.
It means being able to stand alone if needed, without losing myself.

I've come to realize that I am most free when I live in alignment with my own inner knowing, with the creational laws that are written not just in the stars, but in my own spirit-form.
That alignment gives me peace no external liberty can offer.

Now, no matter where I am, I carry my freedom within me.
Even in situations I cannot control, I remain calm, because I know my

thoughts are mine.
My values are mine.
My inner world is sovereign territory, and nothing outside can truly touch it.

This kind of freedom cannot be bought or given.
It must be earned through self-discipline, self-knowledge, and conscious living.
It is the path of responsibility, not escape.
And though it's not always easy, it is worth every step.

In this freedom, I have found strength.
I walk as a free being, not because the world grants it to me, but because I've claimed it from within.

CHAPTER 95:

Psalm 23: 4.

Even when I walk through the darkest valley of my life, I am not afraid, for I know I am not alone.
In alignment with the Creation Energy Teachings, I recognize that the true source of comfort and protection lies not in external powers, but in the eternal presence of my own spirit-form, my inner connection to Creation itself.
The darkness is not something to be feared, but understood, for it is within the darkness that the light of knowledge can be ignited.

The valleys of life, those periods of deep struggle and uncertainty, are part of the natural journey of evolution.
They are not punishments, but necessary stages of growth.
Creation never abandons the human being, for its essence lives within each of us.
When I align with this inner truth, I feel the quiet but unwavering presence of inner guidance.
It is not a divine rod or staff that leads me, it is my consciousness, shaped by natural law, reason, and wisdom.

The rod and staff of ancient symbolism can be understood through the lens of the Creation Energy Teachings as the stabilizing force of inner clarity and the corrective discipline of self-responsibility.
They do not belong to an external god, but are tools I wield myself when I live in harmony with the laws of Creation.
They protect me by guiding me away from ignorance and error, and they comfort me by grounding me in what is real and eternal.

Even in fearsome moments, I draw strength not from outside saviors, but from the knowledge that the Creation is always with me, because it is me.

Its laws are within every breath, every heartbeat, and every thought I have.

There is no distance between myself and Creation.

The separation was only an illusion born from fear and false teachings.

Through inner silence and contemplation, I learn to trust the guidance of my spirit.

It does not speak in thunder or command, but in quiet certainty, helping me discern the right path through my own knowing.

The more I walk this path, the more I understand that no valley is ever permanent, and no night is without its dawn.

The evolution of consciousness is the journey of turning every valley into a peak through awareness.

The Creation Energy Teachings free me from the need to believe in a fearful or comforting god outside myself.

They replace blind faith with inner certainty, superstition with understanding, and helplessness with empowerment.

The true comfort lies not in being watched over by an unseen force, but in being one with the creative force that sustains all life.

Even when everything around me falls into chaos, I can walk in peace if I hold firm to the truth.

My trust is not in miracles, but in the cause-and-effect structure of Creation that allows for learning, growth, and balance.

This is where true protection lies, in understanding the laws of life and living in accordance with them.

This understanding shields the consciousness from despair and confusion.

Every dark valley becomes a teacher when approached with awareness.

Each struggle becomes an opportunity to deepen the connection with the self and Creation.

This is the sacred power of self-realization, and it is available to all who seek it.

I no longer fear the unknown, because I know the eternal part of me cannot be harmed.

And so I walk, not led, but aligned.
Not protected by force, but by knowledge.
Not comforted by fantasy, but by the truth of the eternal rhythm of Creation within me.
In this, I find peace, strength, and the courage to face all things with a calm heart.

CHAPTER 96:

The Surface People.

The surface population of Earth is a patchwork of countless clans.
These clans exist within one another, above and below each other, often in support or in conflict.
Some are well-known, others operate in secrecy, and many remain completely unidentified.
The number of these human groupings continues to grow daily, evolving alongside the shifting needs, ideologies, and hidden agendas of the population.
As it has always been in Earth's long human history, survival and identity are tied to group belonging, just as it is in the animal kingdom.

However, unlike animals that live by instinct, human beings carry a deeper, more complex burden.
We are not merely tribal by nature, we are warlike by design.
This inherited trait is not without origin, it stems from our extraterrestrial ancestry.
Long ago, genetically modified humans were created for war.
These beings, whose remnants live within our genetic memory, were built for conflict, for conquest, and for survival through domination.

Our ancestors did not remain bound to their creators.
Many escaped, journeying across space.
Along the way, some settled temporarily on Mars, while others made their home on the now-destroyed planet Malona.
A catastrophic conflict broke out on Malona, ultimately reducing it to rubble, the remnants of which now form what we know as the Asteroid Belt.

Mars, too, became unstable due to cosmic upheavals, particularly the disruptions caused by the wandering Destroyer Planet.

Eventually, these genetically modified beings, our ancestors, found their way to Earth.
But they arrived not as sages, but as survivors, still carrying the programmed tendencies of war, conflict, and domination.
These tendencies have been inherited by the modern Earth human.
The aggressive nature we see around us today, violence, greed, murder, is not simply social conditioning, but the echo of deep-seated genetic manipulation from a distant past.

Compounding this, Earth itself was once used as a penal colony.
Criminals and undesirables from other worlds were banished here, and now, these same beings continue to reincarnate in human form.
This legacy influences the violent and chaotic conditions we witness daily.
We are not fallen angels, we are, in truth, the so-called barbarians of ancient galactic history.
Our actions have devastated entire solar systems in past incarnations.
That karmic memory still lingers.

Present-day Earth reflects this brutal inheritance.
Murders, shootings, wars, and destruction are not rare exceptions, they are deeply embedded into the human psyche.
We even have colloquial terms like "snapping" to describe sudden outbursts of deadly violence.
This is the harsh truth of our nature.
It is also why peaceful subterranean races, such as the blue- and green-skinned beings beneath the Earth, and the Ocean Dwellers avoid contact with surface humans.
They perceive our aggression and are rightly cautious.

And yet, hope remains.
With awareness and knowledge, a transformation is possible.
The Creation Energy Teachings, brought to us through the spiritual prophet known as BEAM—Billy Eduard Albert Meier, offer a pathway to understanding and renewal.
These teachings explain who we truly are, where we came from, and how we may evolve beyond our destructive tendencies.

230

They remind us that we are not doomed to remain as we are, but have the capacity to change through conscious evolution.

Through these timeless principles and values, many are beginning to awaken to their true, eternal nature.
The war machine identity need not define us any longer.
We can break the cycle of reincarnated violence by realigning ourselves with the Natural-Creational Laws.
And with that shift, a new humanity will rise, one that chooses peace over conflict, truth over ignorance, and unity over tribal fragmentation.

As the enlightened Mothers of the millennium begin to reincarnate again, bringing with them the energy of wisdom and balance, we will witness the slow but certain reemergence of true peace on Earth.
This era of transformation has already begun, and though we still walk amid shadows, the light of knowledge and Creation guides us forward.
Indeed, despite our dark past, we are in good hands.

CHAPTER 97:

Sense of unworthiness.

Human beings on Earth have long struggled with taking full and honest responsibility for their actions. This imbalance arises from a deep-rooted sense of unworthiness and inadequacy, which has been passed down through generations.

Through the Creation Energy Teachings, I've discovered this distorted perception disconnects the human being from their true nature and power.

Instead of recognizing themselves as the creators of their own lives, many Earth humans fall into the illusion that external forces control their fate.

It is a common tendency for people to attribute their successes to some higher power, whether it be a god, a divine plan, or cosmic luck, while shouldering the burden of their failures personally.

This contradictory view fosters confusion and internal division.

In truth, both success and failure are the natural outcomes of one's own thoughts, feelings, decisions, and actions.

The law of cause and effect operates without exception, and each individual is the sole origin of the causes that shape their life.

Through the lens of the Creation Energy Teachings, we understand that we are not puppets of fate or divine whim, but conscious creators of our reality.

The more we attribute power to something outside of ourselves, the more we give up the inner authority necessary for our evolution.

Responsibility is not a punishment, it is the path to liberation.

When the human being claims ownership over every result, whether pleasant or painful, they reclaim their creative power and align with Creation itself.

Feelings of unworthiness stem from ignorance of one's own eternal essence.
The spirit-form within every human being is a fragment of Creation itself, flawless, luminous, and eternal.
It cannot be stained by failure or inflated by success.
These are illusions of the material realm, which can only be overcome through conscious self-recognition and alignment with the truth of one's inner spirit.
To believe one is inadequate is to misunderstand the very nature of being.

Again, Creation does not judge, it only offers possibilities and consequences.
The human being is endowed with free will and the ability to learn through experience.
Mistakes are part of this journey and are not to be condemned, but understood as stepping stones to higher knowledge.
Taking responsibility is not about self-blame or shame, but about clarity, correction, and growth.
Only through this process can true evolution occur.

The teachings emphasize that gratitude should be directed inward, toward one's own spirit-form and consciousness, which together give rise to knowledge, action, and development.
Externalizing this gratitude to imagined deities dilutes the self's role in its own progress.
True reverence is the recognition of the Creational laws and living in harmony with them, not submission to fictional powers.

By internalizing this understanding, the human being gradually dissolves feelings of inferiority and becomes conscious of their innate value.
They no longer see themselves as victims of circumstance or pawns of a divine plan.
Instead, they awaken as responsible co-creators of their lives, constantly

evolving through insight, discipline, and inner strength.
This awakening marks the first true step into conscious living.

When a person takes full responsibility, without praise or blame, they walk the path of the truth.
They cease to fear mistakes because they see them as temporary detours, not personal failures.
They begin to live in balance, recognizing their creative potential and accepting the effects they produce.
This is the path of inner freedom and harmony with Creation.

Ultimately, the journey of the Earth human is not to remain lost in guilt, unworthiness, or superstition,
but to evolve into a being of wisdom, love, and responsibility.
The Creation Energy Teachings guide this transformation by shedding the light of truth on the shadows of self-doubt.
With each lesson integrated and each responsibility embraced, the human being draws closer to their true essence and walks hand in hand with the eternal rhythm of Creation.

CHAPTER 98:

Mental slavery.

I consider myself a very fortunate human being.
From a very young age, I was driven by a deep inner passion to seek the truth, no matter how uncomfortable it might be. This calling to understand life beyond appearances never left me, and it has guided my path even when it led me away from the familiar structures I was raised in.
I grew up within the confines of organized religion, but even then, I could sense something was off.
The teachings preached one thing, yet the actions of those in power revealed something entirely different.

It was particularly striking to observe the clear divide between the wealth of the pastor and the poverty of the congregation.
The disparity was too blatant to ignore.
How could someone claim to represent divine love and justice, yet live lavishly while their followers struggled to eat?
This contradiction was my first real awakening.
It revealed that religion, more often than not, functions as a tool of control and exploitation, rather than as a path to inner freedom and truth.

What troubled me the most was not just the deception itself, but the fact that so many accepted it blindly.
I began to ask myself why the masses couldn't see what was so obvious.
The answer became clear, fear.
Many people are too afraid to question what they've been taught because they've been conditioned to fear punishment from an imaginary, all-seeing God.
It's not logic that holds them back, it's psychological imprisonment.

This fear operates like a disease in the brain.

It paralyzes clear thinking and causes people to abandon their natural curiosity and inner reasoning.

They are terrified of judgment, damnation, and rejection, fictions that have been passed down through generations.

In this way, religion has succeeded in creating a mental framework that enslaves billions, suppressing their ability to recognize their own innate power and responsibility.

The fight for truth is ongoing.

It is a battle that must be waged within ourselves first and then shared with others.

This isn't about converting anyone or forcing them to believe what we do.

It's about awakening the inner drive in others to begin questioning for themselves.

Once that seed is planted, truth has a way of growing in even the most rigid minds.

There is no external god.

There is no omnipotent being sitting in the sky judging our every move.

The concept of "God" is a fabrication, an idea invented by human beings in times of ignorance and fear.

When we accept this truth, it doesn't diminish our worth, it elevates it.

It means that we, as human beings, are responsible for our own lives, for our own evolution, and for the fate of our world.

Only when we discard these ancient illusions can we begin to see each other clearly.

We are not separate tribes or enemies.

We are not divided by race, religion, or ideology unless we choose to be.

In reality, we are all one human race, diverse in appearance and expression, but unified in origin and potential.

This is the truth that religion hides and that fear prevents us from embracing.

Mental slavery is the greatest barrier to human unity.

It keeps people locked in cycles of war, prejudice, and spiritual emptiness.

But when we break through those chains, when we see through the

illusions and reclaim our own inner authority, we set ourselves free.
And freedom is the soil from which real love, compassion, and peace can finally grow.

So we must continue this inner and outer work.
Not with anger or hate, but with firm clarity and unshakable resolve.
The more of us who speak and live the truth, the more cracks appear in the wall of ignorance.
And eventually, that wall will fall.
When it does, humanity will finally be ready to unite, not under the false banner of religion, but through the shared recognition of our true, equal, and eternal nature.

CHAPTER 99:

The Lease.

No one owns anything.
Everything is on a 100-year lease.
And even that is generous.
We come here with nothing in our hands, and when it's time to
go, we leave the same way, empty-handed.
This is the truth that most people avoid because it collapses the
illusions they've built their entire lives around.
But it's also the very truth that sets us free.

The world has confused possession with purpose.
Ownership is a temporary illusion.
Whether it's a house, land, money, or even relationships, nothing belongs
to us.
It is all lent, for a time, so that we may learn, experience, and evolve.
The Creation doesn't give anything permanently to any individual.
It provides everything in cycles, birth, death, rise, fall, inhale, exhale.
The wise one flows with the rhythm and does not cling.

Creation itself has no desire to possess.
It simply unfolds.
It radiates.
It expresses through us.
So what are we doing trying to cling to something that was never ours?
The hands that grasp are the same hands that will one day loosen.
The more we cling, the more we suffer.
But the one who lets go and lives with awareness, that one begins to taste
the peace of the Infinite.

If we see clearly, we are only stewards, not owners.
Stewards of time, of space, of resources, of relationships.
We are here to use, to care for, and to pass along what was once passed to us.
Every generation inherits what the previous one borrowed.
And just like a caretaker, we will one day be asked to hand it all back.
The only thing we truly leave behind is the condition of our consciousness.

The one who understands this becomes humble.
They no longer build castles in the sand of impermanence.
They do not call a thing "mine" with the arrogance of permanence.
Instead, they live in gratitude.
Every breath becomes a gift.
Every moment becomes sacred.
The temporary becomes meaningful, not because it lasts forever, but because it doesn't.

To lease something means to use it wisely.
If we know we only have 100 years, or much less, why waste even a second chasing the illusion of ownership?
Why poison the psyche with greed, envy, or pride over things that are already slipping through our fingers?
The Creation doesn't count what we possess.
It watches how we live.
How we love.
How we grow.

In truth, it is better to lose everything and remain inwardly whole than to gain the world and rot from the inside.
The Earth, the sky, the waters, none of them need us.
But we need them.
They have been here long before us, and they will remain long after.
We're the visitors.
The tenants.
The ones on borrowed time.

And even our body, this beautiful, fragile vessel, is on loan.
It too belongs to the Earth and will return to it.

We are just passing through.
The Spirit-form within, that is what endures.
That is what continues on after the lease is up.
So take care of the body, yes, but don't forget who you are, a timeless flicker of the Eternal, walking through the temporary.

So I walk this Earth as gently as I can.
I use what is given to me, and when it's time to let go, I do so with humility.
I do not own, I only hold.
I do not cling, I care.
I do not possess, I share.
And when the time comes to return everything, including this name, this form, this moment, I will bow my head to the Infinite and return the key.

Chapter 100: Dear racist people.

What you fail to understand is that your desire to live apart from other races is not rooted in pride, strength, or any genuine preservation of heritage.
It is rooted in fear, fear of losing the illusion you've built around yourselves.

You tell yourselves that separation is what you want, that life would be better if you were surrounded only by your own.
But beneath that claim lies a wound you refuse to look at: the insecurity you've carried for so long that you now mistake it for identity.

You've built an entire worldview around the illusion of superiority, clinging to a system that hands you unearned advantages and then convinces you that these advantages are proof of your worth.
You accept this lie because it is easier than confronting the truth.

But deep inside, you know that illusion is all you have.
Without it, you would have to face yourselves without the shield of entitlement that has protected your self-image for generations.

The painful reality is this: you are not racist because you are strong or confident.
You are racist because you are weak, fragile, and terrified of facing your own inadequacies.

In a world constructed by white men for white men, you have confused your privilege with actual value.
You think that standing on top of a tilted system means you climbed there yourself, but deep down, you know you didn't.

You have mistaken dominance for confidence and control for character.
You imagine yourselves as powerful, but your power only exists in spaces where you are protected from real challenge.

Yet none of this fills the emptiness you feel inside.
No amount of hate, exclusion, or imagined superiority fixes the loneliness that comes from never truly knowing who you are without racism propping you up.

That emptiness drives you.
It fuels the lashing out, the anger, the desperate attempts to maintain a hierarchy that only exposes how little you think of yourselves.
Equality terrifies you because it reveals the truth you work so hard to bury, that you are just human.

And that terrifies you more than anything, to be ordinary, to be insecure, to be lost without the illusion of supremacy carrying you.

If you were truly isolated, living only among your own, your fantasy would collapse under its own weight.
There would be no one left to scapegoat, no one left to blame for your unhappiness or your failures.

All the resentment, all the frustration, all the bitterness you project onto others would have nowhere to go but back into yourself.
And in that silence, it would become clear that the real problem has never been race.

Because the truth you avoid, deny, and run from is this: the misery you feel wasn't placed in you by other people.
It was born inside you, shaped by your own choices, fears, and beliefs.

And when that moment of realization arrives, when you finally understand that the race you've spent your life hating was never the cause of your pain, you will see the truth you've been fleeing from all along.

You were.

CHAPTER 101:

The Law of Return.

The Universe operates under an unchangeable law: whatever energy you put out will return to you, and only to you.

This is the law of causality, the principle that governs all action and consequence.

Nothing is random, and there are no innocent bystanders in the eyes of this law.

If you did not vote for a certain leader, the consequences of their actions cannot truly attach to you, because your energy does not resonate with theirs.

The law is not about politics alone, it is about vibration, alignment, and the frequency you project into the world.

What you give energetically is what comes back to you.

Many people fail to understand this principle.

They assume they will be affected by the choices of others, but the truth is that only those whose energy aligns with the source of action will experience its consequences.

The connection can be conscious, through support or agreement, or unconscious, through shared values, fears, or prejudices.

The Latino community provides an example of this.

Many supported leaders or policies that reflected division among themselves. Some sought separation from newer immigrants, forgetting that their own families were once newcomers.

That judgment and separation generated energy, and what they now experience is the reflection of their own energy returning.

Similarly, among Haitians, support for certain leaders stems from personal motives and perspectives, but the law operates the same way: the energy one projects outward is the energy that returns.
Support aligned with divisive or harmful actions inevitably brings consequences back to the supporter.

On a broader scale, consider Palestine.
Internal division, mistrust, and alignment with external forces have created energy that manifests as suffering.
Until communities unite and recognize themselves as one people, hardship will continue to mirror the energy they collectively project.
External protest or outcry alone cannot change this law.

In all cases, outcomes are never random.
They are precise reflections of the energetic stance one takes.
Leaders, governments, or external events cannot override this principle, the Universe does not judge, it simply returns the energy that has been emitted.

The fundamental truth is clear: you can only harm yourself according to the energy you carry within.
The seeds you sow, through thoughts, actions, or alignment, are the seeds you will harvest.
Personal responsibility is therefore paramount, for the consequences are never elsewhere, only within the mirror of your own energy.

Whether in personal life or on the world stage, the law of return operates with absolute precision.
The Universe does not take sides, reward favoritism, or punish arbitrarily.
It simply mirrors the energy you project, without exception, and this knowledge is the key to understanding the true source of cause and effect in every aspect of existence.

CHAPTER 102:

Arab Brothers and Sisters.

The hour has come for you to awaken, for the challenges facing your communities are serious and urgent.
Do not wait for the world's pity, for real change begins within your own hands.
Strength, unity, and vigilance are the tools that will protect your people and your heritage.

No one will come to solve your problems for you.
You must act together, with wisdom, courage, and purpose.
Communities that are organized, supportive, and aware can respond to crises in ways that ensure survival, dignity, and justice for all.

The lands of the Middle East face threats to their integrity, history, and the well-being of their people.
Recognize these threats clearly, so that you can respond strategically and peacefully, defending your homes and heritage through lawful and humanitarian means.

Look to Palestine and the suffering there, its cries echo across deserts and mountains.
Today, hardship is visible, tomorrow, other communities may face similar struggles if action is not taken.
Solidarity and proactive support are essential to prevent further suffering.

Division has long been a source of weakness.
Old rivalries, misunderstandings, and quarrels among communities have been exploited by forces that benefit from fragmentation.
Unity, dialogue, and reconciliation are the strongest forms of defense.

Set aside every old wound and every barrier that separates you. Stand together as a people bound by shared history, culture, and values. When communities are united, they can respond to challenges with wisdom, resilience, and coordinated action.

The time to act is now. Mobilize your cities, villages, and communities to educate, organize, and advocate peacefully. Humanitarian networks, independent media, and legal and diplomatic efforts are all instruments of meaningful, nonviolent change.

Show the world an Arab region that stands together as a resilient, organized, and compassionate force. Protect your land, your people, and your children's future with steadfastness, solidarity, and intelligence, without resorting to violence.

My heart goes out to all who have suffered. Stand united, care for one another, and work for a future where justice, peace, and human dignity prevail. In solidarity, there is strength, and in unity, there is hope.

CHAPTER 103:

The Uniqueness of Every Life.

N o two lives in this universe are the same, and neither are the lessons that each human being is meant to learn. Every soul is unique, and every path is shaped by forces and experiences that cannot be replicated.
Life is not a competition, it is an individual journey designed for growth and evolution.

Just like snowflakes, every life path is distinct, molded by personal experiences, thoughts, and inner development.
No two journeys follow the same pattern, and no two challenges unfold in the same way.
Each human being carries a path that is uniquely theirs, with lessons tailored to their own growth.

What one person is meant to experience cannot be compared to the journey of another.
Each life carries its own timing, purpose, and set of struggles.
Success, failure, joy, or sorrow cannot be measured on a universal scale, because the significance of each event is defined by the individual soul experiencing it.

Titles, wealth, or positions of power do not change the fundamental equality of all human beings.
No matter how high someone rises in the eyes of the world, they are still subject to the same laws of life, the same emotional and spiritual challenges that define the human experience.

Whether someone is known as the richest person on Earth or holds the highest political office, their life is not exempt from struggle.

Elon Musk and Donald Trump, for instance, may appear to possess everything externally, but they face the same inner challenges, uncertainties, and growth opportunities as any other human being.

Outer success does not equate to inner peace.
Happiness is not found in wealth, fame, or power, but in the condition of the inner self.
One may live simply and feel content, while another may live in luxury and feel lost, unfulfilled, or disconnected.
The external world reflects the state of the inner being.

If one were to truly understand the lives of the so-called powerful or rich, it becomes clear that their challenges are merely different, not better or worse, than those of ordinary people.
Each life is designed to teach what the inner being needs, not to impress the world.
Recognizing this diminishes the need to compare oneself with others.

When this truth is fully embraced, envy and feelings of inferiority fade.
People begin to honor their own lives for what they are, appreciating the unique lessons and experiences that shape their growth.
Value is no longer determined by what society praises, but by the depth of understanding, awareness, and development within.

Cherishing one's life, regardless of external appearances, is a sign of true inner strength.
Living with awareness, accepting one's journey, and recognizing that each life is sacred because of what it becomes, this is the path to freedom, fulfillment, and growth.
Every life matters, not for what it owns, but for the evolution it achieves.

CHAPTER 104:

Truth Seekers.

Truth seekers, this path is not an easy one, but it is a journey that will ultimately be victorious.
The pursuit of truth demands courage, patience, and unwavering commitment.
It is not a path for those seeking comfort or convenience, but for those willing to face the shadows of ignorance and self-deception.

Each step toward truth may feel like a struggle against the current, as if the tide itself resists your progress.
Yet it is precisely this struggle that strengthens the spirit and clarifies the mind.
Every challenge encountered along the way is a lesson, every obstacle a guidepost, shaping those who persist into resilient carriers of light and understanding.

The power of truth cannot be silenced.
Even in moments when it seems ignored, rejected, or attacked, truth continues to flow, weaving its influence into the fabric of existence.
Those who embody and share it are already shaping the future, often in ways unseen and unacknowledged, yet profoundly effective.

Keep sharing truth, no matter how small or insignificant the effort may seem.
Every word spoken, every action aligned with truth, sends ripples through the consciousness of humanity.
Even a single seed planted in awareness can grow into a forest of understanding over time.

The world is in desperate need of voices that rise above deception and illusion.

Humanity has slumbered too long under the influence of lies and falsehoods, blind to the greater reality that surrounds them.

It is the role of truth seekers to illuminate that reality, to awaken others from their deep and prolonged sleep.

Never feel isolated on this path, for you are not alone.

Though your efforts may seem unseen, there are countless others walking alongside you in spirit, each carrying their own spark of awareness.

Together, these sparks form a larger flame, a collective light that cannot be extinguished.

You are the trailblazers, the ones who walk ahead to carve a path for others to follow.

Your courage and persistence lay the foundation for generations yet to come, providing guidance and inspiration to those who will walk this road after you.

Even if the world cannot yet recognize the fire you carry, trust that it is igniting a path for future understanding.

Each act rooted in truth contributes to the awakening of consciousness across the globe, even in ways invisible to the eye.

Truth seekers are never abandoned.

You are the pillars of the awakening yet to come, the living proof that knowledge, courage, and integrity endure.

By holding steady in your pursuit, you ensure that the light of truth will continue to shine, long after the shadows of ignorance have faded.

CHAPTER 105:

Like a Tape Recorder.

T he human being can be likened to a tape recorder that only functions during the span of life.
While alive, every thought, emotion, action, and experience is imprinted upon the consciousness, forming the unique recording of that particular existence.
Each decision, each word spoken, and each lesson learned becomes part of that living record.

However, when death arrives, the recorder ceases to function.
The physical body, which served as the instrument of expression and experience, no longer operates.
Just as a recorder stops when its power source is removed, so too does the human personality fall silent when the body perishes.
The recording, the memories and experiences, ends with it.

When we close our eyes in our final moment, it is not an end but a transition.
Just as night gives way to dawn, a new life soon begins.
The spirit-form, eternal and indestructible, continues on its journey, preparing to animate a new body, a new life, and a new personality.

Yet this new existence begins without memory of the last.
The new personality awakens as a blank tape, untouched and ready to record new experiences.
Nothing from the old personality's recording is carried forward, no memories, no attachments, no personal identity.
The past remains where it belongs: in the past.

This forgetting is not a loss but a necessity.
If the new life carried the burdens and memories of countless former existences, confusion would overwhelm the mind.
Each life must begin anew, with clarity and openness, so the process of learning and evolving can continue unimpeded.

The spirit-form, however, does not forget.
It absorbs the essence of every experience, the wisdom, the understanding, the growth, and integrates it into its timeless evolution.
Though the human memory is wiped clean, the spirit quietly carries forward the distilled knowledge gained through all previous lives.

Thus, the true continuity of existence lies not in personal remembrance but in the ongoing refinement of consciousness.
Each new life is a step forward in this infinite journey, shaped by the inner progress made through past learning.

We are, in essence, new recordings upon an ancient, eternal device.
Every lifetime adds to the silent evolution of the spirit-form, contributing to its wisdom even as each individual personality fades away like the echo of a song once played.

In this understanding, death loses its sting and life gains its meaning.
For though the tape is erased, the essence of what was learned endures, carried onward in the eternal rhythm of creation itself.

CHAPTER 106:

Truth Is Liberation.

Nearly everything I once accepted as truth eventually revealed itself to be false or incomplete. The structures I trusted, the beliefs I held, and the assumptions I carried, all of them began to crumble under the weight of deeper understanding.

This unraveling was not pleasant, nor was it quick, it stripped away the comforts of ignorance and demanded that I face life as it truly is.

The process of awakening to truth is rarely smooth.
It requires persistence, courage, and the willingness to confront everything you once thought you knew.
For decades, I immersed myself daily in the teachings of Herald Billy that spoke to the essence of life and existence.
Slowly, layer by layer, they guided me through the fog of illusion toward a clearer perception of reality.

The struggle was real, yet the reward immeasurable.
For in truth, I discovered something that belief could never provide: certainty grounded in direct knowing.
The truth does not flatter or soothe the ego, it liberates it from its own delusion.
Every falsehood that fell away brought with it a new sense of freedom and peace.

Through this inner journey, I came to see that truth transforms everything it touches.
It dissolves the illusions of importance, fear, and dependency.
When truth takes root, nothing can truly impress or disappoint you

anymore, because you begin to see things simply as they are.
Life reveals itself as neutral, balanced, and deeply purposeful beyond the noise of human opinion.

In this understanding, illusions lose their power.
You no longer chase fleeting highs or sink into temporary lows.
Instead, you dwell in a calm clarity that is not swayed by the external world.
The mind becomes light, and the spirit breathes freely, unburdened by false notions of who you are or what you must become.

Truth, in its purest form, is liberation.
It frees you from the bondage of others' expectations and from the endless pursuit of validation.
You begin to live from within, guided by your own consciousness rather than the dictates of belief or conformity.
The opinions of others lose their grip, for you stand firmly in the knowing of yourself.

In this state, you realize that control is an illusion.
You cannot shape others to your will, nor can they shape you.
What remains within your power is yourself, your thoughts, your actions, your intentions.
This recognition is not limitation but empowerment, for it anchors your life in authenticity and self-responsibility.

To live in truth is to experience freedom of the highest order.
It grants the courage to face life without masks and the wisdom to act without pretense.
You no longer seek truth outside yourself, for you carry it within as a living awareness that guides every step.

Seek truth and knowledge, not beliefs and fantasies.
For belief binds the mind, while truth sets it free.
The one who walks this path becomes a true human being, peaceful, self-aware, and in harmony with life itself.

CHAPTER 107:

Life Makes No Mistakes.

Everything that happens in life unfolds with perfect precision, even when it appears chaotic or unjust. There are no coincidences, no misplaced events, and no errors within the greater flow of existence.

Life, in its boundless wisdom, arranges every moment exactly as it must be, so that consciousness may evolve and truth may emerge.

Every experience, whether joyous or painful, serves a higher purpose within the eternal cycle of becoming.

What we often call mistakes are but lessons in motion, guiding us toward deeper understanding.

The thread of creation does not falter or stray, it moves in harmony with laws that are absolute and unfailing.

The unfolding of events is not separate from the present moment.

What we call the future already exists in potential form, contained within the now.

Each decision, each action, and each breath draws it into visible reality.

In truth, the past, present, and future are one continuous act of creation.

When this understanding dawns, a great peace begins to settle within.

You no longer struggle to control or resist life's currents, for you see that everything occurs in perfect timing.

Doubt gives way to trust, and anxiety transforms into calm acceptance.

You begin to live in alignment with the flow rather than in conflict with it.

This insight does not lead to passivity but to clarity.
To know that life makes no mistakes is to act with awareness and inner balance.
Every thought, word, and deed becomes a conscious expression of harmony with the truth of existence.
Nothing is wasted, and nothing is meaningless.

Within this recognition lies the true nature of free will.
Freedom is not about defying destiny but about embracing it with open eyes and an awakened mind.
Every choice you make arises from who and what you are in that precise moment, and thus it could not have been otherwise.

The wise human does not seek to escape their path but to walk it with mindfulness.
They understand that even so-called failures are part of a grander design that leads toward growth and self-realization.
Through awareness, free will becomes the conscious participation in the evolution of one's own spirit.

This is the peace that comes from knowing that life itself is never wrong.
The storms of existence may shake you, but they do not break you, for you recognize their necessity.
You move through life with patience, courage, and faith in the silent intelligence that governs all things.

To live with this understanding is to live as a free and peaceful human being, one who acts without fear, loves without condition, and accepts without resistance.
In this state, harmony with Creation is no longer an ideal to seek but a reality to live.

CHAPTER 108:

All is one.

A ll is one in truth, and any sense of separation exists only in the thoughts and perceptions of the human mind. The divisions that humanity clings to, of race, religion, nation, or belief, are illusions created by misunderstanding.
In reality, there is no "other," only the infinite expression of Creation manifesting through countless forms.
To see this clearly is to recognize that every being, seen and unseen, is part of the same whole.

When this understanding awakens within a person, love for others flows naturally and effortlessly.
It is not a love that must be forced, taught, or earned, it is the natural expression of unity.
To love one another is not a moral duty, but the spontaneous recognition of our shared essence.
When the illusion of division fades, love becomes as effortless as breathing, and compassion replaces judgment.

The illusion of separation dissolves in the light of awareness, leaving only the pure simplicity of connection.
Every act of kindness, every moment of understanding, becomes a reflection of Creation's harmony.
When one no longer sees themselves as separate from the whole, conflict loses its meaning, and peace arises as the most natural state of being.

Through the teachings of Billy Meier, I have come to see and experience this reality for myself.
These teachings do not demand belief, but understanding, the kind that emerges from one's own reflection and observation.

They reveal that oneness is not an abstract idea or a spiritual ideal, but the very structure of existence itself, evident in every cell, every star, every breath.

I recognize now that the oneness of all existence is not a distant goal to be reached someday, but a living truth already within me.
It is not something to chase or to worship, but to awaken to.
Each moment that I live in harmony with this truth, I align more deeply with the creative laws of the universe.
This awareness transforms how I see myself, and how I move through the world.

Because of this understanding, I feel a deep sense of fulfillment and inner strength.
It is not pride in the egoic sense, but the quiet certainty that comes from knowing one stands in truth.
To live in the awareness of oneness is to live in peace with all life, human, animal, and nature alike.
It is to act not out of superiority, but out of responsibility toward the whole.

Dear Earth people, there exists no enemy we did not create ourselves.
Every act of hatred, every conflict, every war begins first in the mind, in the illusion that we are separate from one another.
The external enemies we fight are the shadows of our internal ignorance.
When we heal the division within, the outer conflicts lose their power.

All true change must come from within.
It is not achieved through laws, weapons, or movements, but through the transformation of consciousness.
When each person takes responsibility for their own thoughts, emotions, and actions, the world changes without force.
The outer world is merely the reflection of the inner one, heal the inner, and the outer follows.

Do not judge, change.
Judgment divides, but change unites.
To judge another is to misunderstand yourself, for the faults you condemn in others are reflections of your own unhealed parts.

Instead of judging, become the example of what you wish to see.
Live the truth you know.
In doing so, you contribute to the awakening of humanity, one conscious thought, one peaceful act at a time.

CHAPTER 109:

At the deepest level.

At the deepest level, there is no real difference between Christians, Muslims, and myself. Beneath the surface of words, rituals, and traditions lies the same yearning for truth, the same search for meaning, and the same desire to live in alignment with that which is eternal. Each of us, in our own way, seeks to understand the nature of existence and our relationship to it.

In essence, we are all students of the same truth, though the forms through which we pursue it may differ.

Each of us is devoted to following the teachings of the Herald, the messenger of truth who appears in every age to guide humanity toward knowledge and peace.

These messengers have spoken in different languages and lived in different cultures, yet their essence has always been one and the same: to reveal the eternal laws and recommendations of Creation.

It is this lineage of truth-bringers that connects the teachings across time.

Yet the difference arises in the fact that the original teachings of Jmmanuel and Mohammed were never written down by their own hand. Their words, once pure and clear, were entrusted to others who, though well-intentioned, altered them over time.

Translation, interpretation, and political manipulation reshaped the message until the truth became buried beneath centuries of dogma and control.

What remains in the scriptures of today is a shadow of what once was.

Since most people of their time were illiterate, the oral transmission of knowledge left room for distortion.

Over generations, myths replaced wisdom, and faith replaced knowing. The teachings that once spoke of personal responsibility, spiritual evolution, and unity with Creation became twisted into systems of belief that demanded obedience and fear.
In this corruption, humanity lost its direct connection to truth.

Now, in the present, the messenger Billy Meier has returned, and for the first time, the true Creation-Energy Teaching is being written down by the teacher himself.
There is no middleman, no interpreter, no prophet rewriting another's words.
What is given now comes directly from the source of truth, clear and undiluted.
This marks a turning point in human history, the restoration of what was once lost.

This is the teaching I follow.
Just as others place their trust in the Bible or the Quran, I place mine in the Goblet of the Truth.
Yet I do not do so out of belief, but out of recognition.
I have read, reflected, and experienced the truth within these words, and through them, I have come to understand the workings of Creation.
My trust is not blind faith, it is the certainty that arises from personal realization.

I do not consider myself religious, for my path is not one of belief but of knowing.
Religion asks for devotion to an external authority, but knowing requires the awakening of one's own consciousness.
The path I walk is guided by the immutable laws of the universe, the law of cause and effect, of balance, and of evolution.
It is the natural order of Creation itself, untouched by human ambition or distortion.

Through this path, I have come to recognize myself as my own god, not in arrogance, but in understanding that I am a part of Creation, and Creation is within me.
To live in harmony with this truth is to act in awareness of the power and responsibility that come with it.

The divine is not a distant being to be worshipped, but the living energy that animates every form of life.

The distorted teachings of religion keep their followers bound in chains, feeling small and powerless, waiting for an outside god to save them.
But the true teaching reveals freedom, the freedom to know that salvation is self-created through conscious evolution.
The divine spark is already within us, waiting to be recognized.
We are not servants of Creation, we are its living expression.
In this knowing, one no longer worships, but lives, as a conscious co-creator in the eternal unfolding of life.

CHAPTER 110:

Same human family.

We all belong to the same human family, bound not by divisions of color or creed, but by the essence of life itself that flows through every being on Earth.
Beneath the surface differences that the eyes perceive lies a shared ancestry that connects us all.
No matter where one is born or what language one speaks, we are threads of the same vast tapestry, woven together by Creation.

Not a single person on this planet carries DNA that is exclusive to any one race.
The idea of racial purity is a human invention, an illusion that collapses under the weight of scientific truth.
The fact that every person can intermix and bring forth new life stands as undeniable proof of our shared origin.
Our diversity is not separation, it is expression, the many colors of one living humanity.

Today you may live as a white man, yet in another life, you may return as a black man or woman, or as someone born to a culture you once misunderstood.
The spirit within you does not belong to any race, nation, or religion.
It is timeless, moving through forms and faces as it evolves through experience.
To recognize this is to see beyond the temporary and understand the eternal unity of all life.

If humanity could truly grasp this reality, much of racism would dissolve into nothingness.

The illusion of superiority would vanish once people understood that the same consciousness animates every being.

The hatred that divides nations and the arrogance that sustains oppression would lose their meaning.

What remains would be the truth, that in harming another, we harm ourselves.

Yet, the road ahead remains long.

Many still cling to outdated beliefs and false hierarchies that feed fear and separation.

These ideas have been passed down through generations, shaping cultures and poisoning hearts.

They are the chains that bind humanity to its lowest instincts, preventing the emergence of true spiritual maturity.

Still, there is hope.

For every person who awakens to the truth of oneness, the darkness of ignorance loses ground.

With each act of understanding, each gesture of compassion, the collective consciousness of humanity shifts closer to balance.

Evolution may be slow, but it is steady, and no illusion can resist truth forever.

Patience is required, for transformation does not happen overnight.

The wounds of division run deep, and healing demands both courage and humility.

Each person must begin within, to cleanse the thoughts that separate, to challenge the biases inherited, and to see every other human as a reflection of themselves.

This is the quiet work that builds a peaceful world.

Persistence is equally necessary.

It is not enough to simply know that we are one, we must live it in our daily actions.

The true test of understanding lies in how we treat others, especially those different from ourselves.

Each choice, no matter how small, either strengthens or weakens the unity of the human family.

The day will come when humanity rises above its illusions of separation.

When the colors of skin will be seen as variations of beauty rather than measures of worth.

When the idea of race will be remembered only as an ancient misunderstanding.

On that day, the human family will stand together as it was always meant to, as one people, sharing one home, guided by one eternal spirit.

CHAPTER 111:

The inner being.

The inner being is the silent foundation of who you are, untouched, unshaken, and eternal beneath the surface of every experience.
No matter what unfolds around you, no one can truly affect this inner core without your permission.
The storms of life may rage, people may speak or act unjustly, yet your true self remains beyond their reach.
To remember this is to reclaim your strength and your peace.

The outer world may appear chaotic, constantly shifting between order and confusion, harmony and conflict.
Yet your greatest power lies not in trying to control these fluctuations, but in guarding the stillness within.
When you anchor yourself in that inner stillness, the noise of the world loses its hold.
You become the calm observer rather than the restless participant in every storm.

You always have the choice to remain untouched within, even when everything outside seems unstable.
This choice is not denial or indifference, it is wisdom.
It is the understanding that your inner state determines how you experience life, not the other way around.
In this awareness, peace becomes something you carry with you, not something you chase in the world.

It is natural to express your thoughts and opinions, to engage with others and stand by your values.

But it is equally important to avoid taking matters personally.
When you take offense or react from pride, you open the door for others to disturb your inner balance.
True strength is not found in winning arguments, but in remaining centered when others lose themselves in theirs.

When you let external circumstances dictate your emotions, you hand over your peace.
Every time you allow anger, frustration, or fear to dominate your mind, you give away a piece of your freedom.
Instead, pause, breathe, and remember that you can choose how to respond.
The power to remain calm is not weakness, it is mastery.

Recognize what is beyond your control and release it.
Trying to force what cannot be changed only creates unnecessary turmoil within.
Life flows more harmoniously when you stop resisting what is and focus instead on what you can guide, your thoughts, your reactions, your understanding.
Surrendering control is not defeat; it is liberation.

The key is to meet each situation with neutrality.
Neutrality does not mean apathy, but clarity, seeing things as they are without distortion.
It allows you to act with reason rather than impulse, to speak with wisdom rather than reaction.
Through neutrality, you maintain your balance even in the face of extremes.

By not allowing anger, fear, or attachment to govern your reactions, you preserve your inner peace.
Emotions are natural, but they are not meant to rule you.
When you observe them without clinging or resisting, they pass like clouds across a clear sky, leaving your consciousness untouched and luminous.

This calm, centered state is what sustains true peace, regardless of how turbulent the outside world may appear.

It is the realization that your serenity does not depend on others, nor on circumstances, but on the harmony between your thoughts and your inner being.

In this harmony, you discover freedom, the unshakable peace that no force in the world can take away.

CHAPTER 112:

Knowledge.

Knowledge is not something that can be rushed, nor can it be claimed by mere association.
It is not a title, a belief, or a collection of memorized ideas.
True knowledge is an ongoing process, one that unfolds through patience, introspection, and honest confrontation with oneself.
It cannot be borrowed from another, nor inherited through proximity to truth, it must be earned through one's own inner labor.

True knowledge requires time, reflection, and the willingness to let it shape who you are.
It demands humility, because real learning often begins where certainty ends.
To know truth is not to possess it, but to allow it to possess you in the sense that it reshapes your thoughts, your conduct, and your relationship with all life.
Those unwilling to be transformed by what they know will always remain at the surface, mistaking familiarity for understanding.

To merely know of something is not to truly understand it.
Understanding goes far beyond the collection of facts or the repetition of words, it requires living in alignment with what is known.
The difference between knowing and understanding is the same as the difference between light and warmth: one illuminates, the other sustains.
Without lived practice, even the most profound truth remains lifeless within the mind.

For example, even among those who have been introduced to the truth of Creation and the Universal Consciousness, where everything is interconnected as one, many are Trump supporters, a man full of hate and racism.

This paradox reveals the chasm between knowledge and wisdom, between exposure to truth and the embodiment of it.

The teachings of Creation call for unity and peace, yet some who have studied them still cling to fear, separation, and false strength.

One would expect that with such sacred knowledge, they would naturally lean toward peace, equality, and respect for all human beings.

That they would see beyond illusions of superiority and reject any leader who thrives on division and deceit.

Yet, this is not always the case.

The mind may learn the words of truth, but the heart must accept their meaning, and that is where many falter.

Their alignment with a man who thrives on division and insecurity reveals the contradiction between what they claim to know and what they truly embody.

It is one thing to read about oneness, and another to live as though all beings are one.

This hypocrisy exposes how easily truth can be used as decoration, a badge of enlightenment worn to hide inner blindness.

Real knowledge does not coexist with deceit or hate, it dissolves them.

Reflecting on this has shown me that knowledge by itself is never enough.

It can guide, inspire, and awaken, but without personal transformation, it remains incomplete.

The world is full of people who speak of truth yet live in contradiction to it.

True knowing requires honesty, the kind that dismantles illusions of self-importance and forces one to confront their own ignorance.

Knowledge must become more than an idea held in the mind; it must be lived, practiced, and integrated into one's being.

Each thought, word, and action must reflect the principles one claims to understand.

When knowledge moves from theory to practice, from belief to behavior, it begins to reveal its true purpose, not to elevate one above others, but to awaken the consciousness within all.

Only then does knowledge transform into wisdom, and only then does it shape a person in a way that truly reflects the truth they claim to uphold.

Wisdom is not what one knows, it is what one becomes through the continual effort to live truthfully.

It is the harmony between thought and deed, between learning and being. And it is in that harmony that the real essence of Creation can finally be experienced.

CHAPTER 113:

The miserable human being named Trump.

The miserable human being named Trump is not an exception, he is the mirror of America's soul.
He did not emerge from nowhere, nor did he seize power through brilliance or virtue.
He rose because the sickness that created him was already deeply rooted in the heart of America.
He is not a mistake of history, but its inevitable outcome, a reflection of what festers beneath the flag's illusion of greatness.

He stands as the living embodiment of what this country has become: selfish, hateful, arrogant, uneducated, greedy, classless, heartless, insecure, and above all, racist.
Every cheer, every defense, every blind justification for his cruelty exposes the moral decay that runs through the veins of this nation.
He is not merely a man, he is a symptom of a deeper rot that millions have chosen to ignore.

You may despise him, but in truth, you despise what you have allowed yourselves to become.
The outrage toward him is an act of denial, a way to separate yourselves from the ugliness you helped sustain.
He exists because people have traded compassion for spectacle, truth for convenience, and decency for tribal victory.

He is the creation of a people who worship ignorance and celebrate cruelty as if they were virtues.
The chants of "USA! USA! USA!" are not cries of unity or strength, they are hollow echoes of a people desperate to convince themselves that patriotism can hide moral collapse.

When ignorance becomes entertainment and cruelty becomes policy, you no longer have a nation, you have a circus run by its loudest clowns.

Don't judge him, look at yourself.
Look at what you've tolerated, encouraged, and silently supported.
The hatred you condemn in him is the same hatred you excuse in your family, your politics, your media, and your silence.
Every lie you let pass, every injustice you overlook, every truth you refuse to face has kept him alive and thriving.

This is who you are as a society that thrives on division, builds power through deception, and finds comfort in the suffering of others.
You have mistaken cruelty for strength, ignorance for authenticity, and manipulation for leadership.
You have built a culture that rewards the loudest voice, not the wisest one.
And in doing so, you created a world where truth no longer matters, only spectacle does.

The arrogance you see in him lives in you.
The hate you hear from him echoes your silence.
The greed that drives him feeds on your complicity.
He is not separate from you, he is the sum of your collective cowardice, the portrait of a people too afraid to face themselves.

He is the face of your collective failure, the proof that a nation without wisdom becomes its own disease.
This country didn't just produce him, it protected him, rewarded him, and called him a leader.
In him, America sees its reflection: loud, broken, proud, and blind.

So if you wish to condemn him, first have the courage to confront the truth, he is you.
You made him, you sustained him, and you excused him.
Until that changes, this nation will keep birthing new versions of him again and again.
You are miserable, and until you face that misery, there will be no cure.

CHAPTER 114:

When people can't eat, they eat the rich.

When people can't eat, they eat the rich.
This is not a slogan born of envy, but a warning written in the blood of history.
Whenever the masses are pushed beyond the limits of survival, when the hunger for food and fairness collides, the powerful are the first to fall.
Every age has witnessed this cycle, the moment when luxury mocks suffering, and the balance of existence demands to be restored.

Throughout time, civilizations have collapsed under the weight of their own greed.
When the few hoard what the many have earned, when prosperity is privatized and misery becomes public, the very foundation of society begins to rot.
No empire, no dynasty, no government built upon exploitation has ever withstood the hunger of its people.
The pattern is ancient and undeniable, the more a system takes, the closer it moves toward its own destruction.

But hunger is not only of the stomach.
It is of justice, dignity, and the right to live without humiliation.
A person deprived of nourishment feels the sting of inequality not just in the body, but in the soul.
This hunger grows quietly at first, buried beneath obedience and fear, until one day it erupts, consuming everything in its path.
It begins with whispers, protests, and then flames.

When that hunger becomes unbearable, it does not discriminate, it devours palaces and towers alike.
Those who feast while others starve become symbols of the injustice that birthed the rage.
The illusion of wealth as untouchable power begins to crumble.
The gold that once gleamed as security turns to ash in the hands of those who thought themselves gods.

The poor possess no weapons but their numbers, and that is all they need.
When united by desperation, they become a force that no army, no wall, no propaganda can contain.
History's revolutions were never born of ideology alone, they were born of empty stomachs and broken promises.
Hunger, when collective, becomes a storm no ruler can escape.

The rich may build fortresses, hire guards, and purchase politicians, but none of it can silence the voice of starvation.
When a population can no longer afford food, shelter, or hope, it does not rise out of greed, it rises out of instinct.
To live becomes the only law.
And those who hoarded life's essentials become the first targets of that instinctive fury.

So when people can't eat, they eat the rich, not because they want to, but because they have been given no other choice.
It is not rebellion for the sake of chaos; it is nature's correction against imbalance.
It is life reclaiming itself from the clutches of excess and indifference.
The rich who ignore this truth do not understand that their comfort is sustained by a fragile illusion, one that ends the moment the hungry stop waiting.

Those who sit atop mountains of gold should remember: no throne is safe when the people below it are starving.
Hunger is the great equalizer, indifferent to wealth, title, or lineage.
When the human need to survive surpasses fear, nothing built on greed can endure.
You've been warned.

CHAPTER 115:

The grand play of life.

Life, in its deepest and most profound essence, functions very much like a grand and intricate play, one whose stage is the material world, and whose actors are each of us, clothed in temporary identities.

We enter into this world much like performers, stepping onto the stage of existence to play out roles chosen for our learning and development.

These roles vary from life to life, from scene to scene, and they are never the same.

One moment we are teachers, the next we are students.

One day we are strong and confident, the next we are fragile and uncertain.

Through each role, we are not meant to become the character, but to evolve the spirit behind it.

Every experience, every encounter with another human being, and every internal struggle we face is a carefully placed moment in this play, designed not to define us permanently, but to shape and awaken us.

The script of life is written by the impulses of our inner consciousness and the laws of Creation, which bring to us the exact lessons we need for the development of our awareness.

When one act of learning ends, we step back, rest, reflect, and prepare for the next.

This may happen over the course of a single lifetime or across many, but the rhythm of preparation, performance, and transformation is a timeless one.

Once an episode concludes, be it a stage of life, a challenge overcome, or even an entire incarnation, we return to the metaphysical changing room of existence.

There, the deeper part of us, the spirit-form, does not rest idly but instead integrates what was learned, readying itself for the next journey. This cycle of birth, experience, reflection, and rebirth is as natural as the rising and setting of the sun.

And knowing this cycle intimately, not merely as a belief but through inner observation and understanding, has forever changed the way I walk through this life.

These teachings did not merely tell me to be calm or detached, they gave me the tools to understand why things happen the way they do.

I now see that every joy, every pain, every relationship, and every challenge is part of a scene that is here not to defeat me, but to instruct me.

By choosing to observe rather than attach, I have freed myself from the emotional chaos that once ruled my mind.

I have learned to watch my thoughts instead of being ruled by them.

I remain centered in the knowledge that the stage of life is not a trap, it is a mirror, reflecting back to me what I must confront, heal, and ultimately transcend.

I no longer move through life trying to force outcomes or control others. Instead, I flow with the understanding that all things serve the process of evolution, mine and everyone else's.

Each role I play, each lesson I observe, and each truth I uncover brings me closer to the core of who I really am.

I am not here merely to survive, to succeed, or to suffer, I am here to become.

To become wiser, more peaceful, more aligned with the laws of Creation. With every act, the spirit within me grows in consciousness and clarity.

And with each passing moment, I am reminded that I am not the play, I am the one who watches it, who learns from it, and who ultimately outgrows it.

I am a conscious, evolving being on an eternal journey back to truth, back to source, back to myself.

Life, in its deepest unfolding, is a classroom.

Every moment presents itself as a lesson, shaped not by outside forces

alone but by the inner movements of our own thinking.
What appears fixed or absolute often reveals itself as fluid once we examine it with clarity.

Nothing carries the weight of reality until we, within ourselves, give it form.
An experience is simply an event until our thoughts assign meaning to it.
Through this quiet process, the human being turns the invisible into the lived.

Everything we call "real" has already passed through the filter of our consciousness.
We interpret, we define, and we breathe life into what stands before us.
Without this inner participation, the world remains only a possibility, not yet shaped into experience.

In this way, the human being becomes the artist of their own existence.
What we think, we color with feeling, what we feel, we anchor into our lives.
The outer world mirrors the patterns we cultivate within.

Once this truth reveals itself, a quiet empowerment begins to rise.
The chains we once imagined around us start to loosen, not because the world has changed, but because we are no longer mistaking illusions for immovable walls.

With this recognition, we realize that freedom is not something granted, it is something lived from within.
Each thought becomes a step, each insight a door, each moment an opportunity to reshape the direction of our path.

As the human being accepts their role in constructing their reality, responsibility naturally awakens.
Our choices no longer drift in unconsciousness, they become deliberate expressions of our inner structure.

Through this understanding, we can move in life with greater calm.
The storms outside lose their power, for they no longer define us.
We stand rooted in our own clarity, guided by our own direction.

And ultimately, once we embrace this inner authority, we become free to live according to our own quiet desire, no longer pushed by fear, no longer pulled by illusion, but directed by the simple strength of conscious awareness.

CHAPTER 116:

The flow of life.

I
t is not life itself that causes pain, but the resistance to it.
Human beings often create unnecessary suffering by
opposing the natural rhythm of existence.
When thoughts, emotions, or experiences are met with denial or
inner conflict, the harmony of the moment is disturbed, and the
individual distances themselves from the truth of what is.
This resistance becomes a wall, separating one from the clarity
that could otherwise emerge.

The Creation Energy Teaching shows that all events carry meaning,
and every situation, pleasant or difficult, holds a lesson for one's
evolution.
But these lessons are not forced, they are gently revealed when one
becomes still and receptive.
In the state of inner flow, the pressure of resistance dissolves, and what
once seemed like pain transforms into understanding.

By aligning with the flow of life, one stops struggling against the
inevitable. Life unfolds according to the law of causality, cause and effect,
and the more this law is respected, the less friction one experiences.
Those who embrace what comes, without clinging or rejecting, find peace
even in turmoil, because they are grounded in the knowledge that all
things pass and evolve.

To be in flow is not to be passive.
It is to be conscious, clear, and in tune with what is essential.
In the stillness of acceptance, true strength is found. Gratitude is not
something one forces, it arises naturally when one recognizes the value
of each experience.

Even hardship becomes a sacred mirror, showing what must be seen and understood.

The Creation within every human being seeks expansion through learning.
Life is the teacher, and the more one resists its lessons, the more those lessons repeat with increasing intensity.
But once one surrenders, not to fate, but to conscious realization, a deeper intelligence begins to guide.
One becomes aware that growth is not punishment but opportunity.

There is no evolution without challenge.
But it is not the challenge that breaks a person, it is the unwillingness to face it.
When one becomes humble before life, the lessons no longer feel like punishment.
They are understood as the precise experiences needed for the development of consciousness and inner clarity.

To be grateful for life means to recognize that nothing is wasted.
Every encounter, every loss, every moment of silence or confusion is part of a greater unfolding.
It is not about blind optimism but about seeing clearly, what comes, comes for a reason, what leaves, leaves for a reason.
When this is realized, suffering loses its grip.

Life is not a random sequence of events but a purposeful unfolding of causes and consequences, shaped by one's thoughts, actions, and inner state.
By flowing with this understanding, one acts with greater responsibility and mindfulness, knowing that even the smallest movement has impact.
Resistance dissolves as wisdom deepens.

Truly, peace is found not by controlling life, but by flowing with it.
When one flows, one aligns with Creation itself, and in that alignment, there is no room for resistance, only learning, understanding, and gratitude.
In this state, life is not a burden to endure, but a journey to evolve through.

CHAPTER 117:

You.

Y ou are eternal.
Not as an idea, but as a fact rooted in the very laws of the Creation itself.
The spirit-form within you, the true essence of your being, cannot be destroyed.
It is not bound to death or decay, as is the material body.
It exists beyond the confines of flesh, blood, and bone.
The reality is that you are not the body, you are within the body.

That is why you say "my body", because the body is something you possess, not something you are.
It serves as your vessel in this current lifetime.
Through it, you speak, feel, walk, and live.
But you must never confuse this temporary shell with the timeless energy that animates it.
The spirit-form is ancient, older than memory, and will continue to exist long after the present body has returned to the earth.

In this life, you are playing a role.
This personality, with its name, habits, and beliefs, is only a temporary expression of your eternal essence.
Just as an actor wears costumes and speaks lines in a play, you wear this life for a time.
But you are not the role.
You are the one playing it, learning through it, and evolving by way of its experiences.

This knowledge brings clarity.
When you understand that the character you play is not the fullness of

your being, you are freed from attachments and illusions.
The sorrows and victories of this life are passing moments, lessons, not identities.
What remains true is the spirit-form, which carries every experience as a neutral impulse, fueling your evolution toward greater awareness.

After death, you do not disappear.
You do not go to some final judgment or eternal resting place.
Instead, your spirit returns to the spirit-realm, where it rests and processes all that has been learned.
Then, when the time is right, it returns to a new life, in a new form, to continue the journey.
This process is orderly, natural, and governed by the laws of Creation.

Each incarnation is an opportunity.
You come back again and again not because you are being punished, but because you are learning.
Each life presents new challenges, new insights, new growth.
Through joy and pain, you accumulate wisdom.
Through triumphs and errors, you begin to know truth.
And truth is what guides your evolution toward a higher state of consciousness.

The goal is not to become perfect in one life, but to evolve gradually through many.
The Creation is patient, and so must you be.
Everything you experience, every relationship, every hardship, every joy, is part of a larger plan that moves you forward step by step.
The more you live in alignment with this truth, the more peace and clarity you will find.

Do not fear the end of this life.
Fear is born from ignorance of who you really are.
When you know yourself as a part-piece of Creation, fear dissolves.
What is there to fear, when you are infinite?
Death is not the end, but simply the closing of a chapter.
The spirit remains, intact and purposeful, awaiting its next opportunity to grow.

This is the truth.

As the Creation Energy Teaching shows us, you are not the body.
You are not the character.
You are the spirit-form, eternal, undying, ever-evolving.
Learn to live from this awareness.
Let it guide your thoughts, actions, and relationships.
For in this recognition lies freedom, peace, and the purpose of life itself.

CHAPTER 118:

The formula.

The former understanding that a human spiritform would remain in the afterlife for a time calculated by multiplying the age of death by 1.52 is no longer valid.
That formula, once accurate, has been overtaken by the consequences of overpopulation.
In today's world, the frequency of reincarnation has accelerated unnaturally, and this disruption is not the work of Creation, but the result of human ignorance and irresponsibility.

Spiritforms are now reincarnating into new human bodies far too quickly, without the necessary rest and processing time in the beyond. This premature return causes confusion in the consciousness of the new personality, which has not been fully programmed and prepared.
As a result, we are seeing more and more cases where young children are partially recalling moments or feelings from their former lives, which should not be the case under natural circumstances.

These anomalies occur because the complete erasure of the old personality, as well as the proper development of the new one, are being rushed or left incomplete.
Creation itself, being perfect and neutral, does not make mistakes, so the fault lies not in the spiritual process, but in the mismanagement of earthly life by human beings.
We have tampered with the natural flow of life through our overbreeding and refusal to live in alignment with the laws of nature.

It must be understood clearly, the Creation does not interfere with human decisions.
It provides the energy and the evolutionary framework, but the responsibility for right action always lies with the human beings

themselves.

So when we overpopulate the planet, it is not Creation's doing, but our own defiance of the truth and of spiritual law.

One of the most dangerous forces behind this crisis is the religious delusion that commands people to "go forth and multiply," as though the meaning of life were to fill the Earth beyond capacity.

This senseless directive has encouraged breeding without wisdom or restraint, ignoring the delicate balance of nature and evolution.

We are now bearing the fruit of this spiritual ignorance.

Overpopulation is not only causing ecological collapse and global warming, but it is also interrupting the sacred rhythm of reincarnation. When more bodies exist than properly matured spiritforms ready for incarnation, then spiritual confusion, identity mismatches, and emotional instability grow rampant across society.

It is not enough to observe these issues passively.

We must act as stewards of the Earth and correct the mistakes of past generations.

The overpopulation problem is solvable, but only through conscious effort, education, and self-restraint.

We must make space once again for the proper cycle of birth, death, afterlife, and rebirth to unfold naturally.

Billy Meier, alongside the Plejaren, has warned humanity for decades about this crisis.

Their messages are not predictions, but prophecies, warnings that can be averted if we change our behavior.

Unfortunately, most of Earth's population dismisses or ridicules these messages, blind to their own downfall and deaf to the wisdom of the ages.

And so the spiral continues downward.

But those who have eyes to see and ears to hear must not grow discouraged.

Each of us carries the power to change our course, not only for ourselves but for all future generations.

The task is not small, but neither is the spiritform within us.

With knowledge, discipline, and truth, we can restore the balance once more.

CHAPTER 119:

The Great Majority.

T he great majority of human beings on Earth have no true understanding of who they are.
Too often, the inner self remains a distant stranger, unvisited and unexamined.

They move through life wearing identities shaped by fear, hope, belief, and the expectations placed upon them.
These borrowed layers create a mask so convincing that even they cannot see beyond it.

Yet beneath all of that, their real essence remains untouched and unknown to them.
It waits quietly, patient but unheard, beneath the noise of their daily illusions.

Even those who confidently claim self-knowledge often reveal through their actions and reactions that they only know the surface of themselves. Their certainty dissolves the moment life tests them.

They speak of clarity, but it is a clarity built on ideas borrowed from others, not on inner truth gained through honest reflection.
Their foundation is belief, not knowing.

Everywhere I look, I see people convinced that the person they "believe" themselves to be is the person they truly are.
Belief becomes identity, and identity becomes limitation.

They cling to that belief as if it were a lifeline, unaware that the belief itself is the very thing restricting their growth, their insight, and their ability to evolve into something more.

This misunderstanding creates a world full of individuals acting out roles rather than expressing their true inner nature.
Humanity performs itself instead of living itself.

People mistake their thoughts for identity, their emotions for essence, and their beliefs for true understanding.
In doing so, they drift further from the self that exists beneath all temporary states.

In this confusion, many wander through life without ever confronting the deeper question: Who am I beyond what I've been taught to think about myself?
Without that question, all answers remain incomplete.

Few dare to strip away the layers of illusion to discover the quiet reality within.
The process demands courage, honesty, and the willingness to let go of the familiar false self.

Yet, in all my encounters, I have met only one human being who truly showed me something different.
He stood as living proof that inner knowing is not merely an idea, it is a presence.

He didn't introduce himself with words, titles, or claims.
There was no performance, no attempt to be anything for me or for anyone else.

Instead, he recognized me in a way only someone who knows themselves can recognize another.
It felt as though he had met me long before our physical meeting, as if the connection existed beyond ordinary perception.

In that moment, I understood how rare true inner knowing is.
And I realized that until a human being meets themselves fully, they cannot truly meet anyone else.

CHAPTER 120:

I am named Waid.

I n this present incarnation, the name I carry is Waid.
I was born in Haiti, raised within the conditions and
circumstances necessary for my learning and growth.
I attended Collège Canado for high school and later migrated to
the United States, where new chapters of experience awaited.
In the U.S., I studied at York College, and further deepened my
academic journey at the Sorbonne and Université de Nanterre in
France.
Each of these paths played a role in the unfolding of this
character I currently express in this lifetime.

At one point, I became a schoolteacher, feeling the impulse to share
what I had learned and help shape young minds.
But it didn't take long before I recognized that the education system I
was part of was not truly designed to uplift or evolve human beings.
It was more focused on conformity, control, and distraction.
I could not be a participant in something that neglected the inner
development and dignity of the human spirit, so I chose to walk away,
listening instead to the deeper call within me.

This call led me on an inward search.
I no longer sought answers from outer institutions or belief-based
structures.
I searched for truth, pure, timeless, and free of manipulation.
In that quest, I came upon a man named Billy Meier.
His teachings were unlike anything I had come across.
They were direct, factual, grounded in logic and universal law.
From that moment forward, my life was forever changed, not because I
adopted a new belief, but because I began to understand.

Billy's teachings reminded me of something ancient within myself. They taught me about the spirit-form that dwells in every human being, about Creation and the laws that govern all life.
I came to understand that I am not the role I play.
Waid is a character, a necessary experience for this lifetime.
But the essence of who I truly am, the spirit-form within me, is far greater, infinite, and without name or label.

Still, I honor Waid.
I honor the experiences, the suffering, the breakthroughs, and the wisdom gained through this life.

Everything that is true and real, every piece of knowledge and every conscious realization, will remain within my consciousness-block.
It will accompany my spirit through the transition after death and become part of the next incarnation.
Nothing learned is ever lost.

Through Billy Meier's teaching, I came to recognize that belief is an obstacle to truth.
Belief is assumption without evidence, while truth can be tested, lived, and known.
The Creation-energy teachings do not require faith, they require self-responsibility.
I have embraced this responsibility and strive each day to live in accordance with the natural laws of life, of cause and effect, of love, of striving.

I no longer fear death, for I understand that it is merely a transition.
What dies is the name, the body, and the personality.
What continues is the spirit and the accumulation of real knowledge.
I no longer live to prove anything to the world, I live to evolve, to learn, to recognize truth where it reveals itself, and to carry it forward silently within me.

Waid is a role I will one day lay down, just as I have laid down other names in previous lives.
But the journey continues.
The real self, the spirit-form that animates this life, is on an eternal path,

shaped not by wealth, status, or appearance, but by truth, learning, and wisdom.

And with each life, I come one step closer to the timeless oneness with Creation.

So I live this life consciously, with deep gratitude.

I give thanks for Waid and the experiences of this life.

I give thanks for Billy and the teachings he has preserved and passed on.

But above all, I give thanks to the silent, eternal presence of the spirit within me, the true me, who walks forward, lifetime after lifetime, in service to evolution, to truth, and to the light of Creation itself.

Final wisdom.

From what I have come to know through the Creation Energy Teachings, the path to inner and outer balance begins with the conscious decision to prioritize peace and harmony in all aspects of life.

It is not merely a passive state but an active choice made in every moment, especially during times of stress or conflict.

When one seeks peace within, it radiates outward, influencing every interaction and environment.

True peace, according to the teachings, is not dependent on external conditions but arises from the knowledge of one's unity with Creation and its eternal wisdom.

Respect for the freedom of others is a fundamental requirement for maintaining harmony.

Every human being, by nature of their existence, possesses the right to express their thoughts, feelings, and ideas.

Whether or not one agrees with another's opinion is secondary to the realization that freedom of thought and expression is a Creational right.

Disrespecting this principle leads only to division and misunderstanding.

The more we honor each other's voice, the more we grow collectively in consciousness.

Listening is more than the act of hearing words, it is an expression of respect and an acknowledgment of another's inner world.

The teachings remind us that all humans are undergoing their own personal evolution, and by listening deeply and without interruption, we affirm their worth.

In doing so, we also allow our own thoughts to mature before sharing them.

Patience, in this context, is not silence but wisdom in motion.

Each moment of silence is an invitation to self-reflect and to connect more deeply.

Arguments are not battles to be won but doors to new understanding. The Creation Energy Teachings clarify that the desire to "win" stems from ego and insecurity, whereas the desire to understand stems from growth and strength.
When engaged in disagreement, we are presented with the opportunity to evolve by learning another perspective.
If approached with humility and the intent to expand our knowledge, arguments can become sacred exchanges rather than destructive encounters.

Every single interaction we have is a mirror and a lesson.
Even the most casual conversation carries potential insights, if one remains open to them.
The Universe teaches through people, through events, and even through silence.
The moment we assume we have nothing more to learn is the moment we shut the door to our evolution.
The teachings emphasize that wisdom flows continuously to those who keep their inner vessel open and willing.

Kindness and respect are not ideals to be practiced only when convenient, they are foundational to the nature of a truly evolved human.
When we treat others with dignity, we affirm our own.
Likewise, when we allow mistreatment without boundaries, we teach others how little we value ourselves.
According to the principles of the spirit-teaching, each human must teach others how to treat them through the example of self-respect.
Only then can mutual respect flourish.

To express one's inner world authentically is to experience the freedom that is one's birthright.
We were not born to suppress our truth or to hide our light behind fear.
Genuine communication allows the spirit to breathe and strengthens the connection between thought, feeling, and action.
The Creation does not conceal its essence, it expresses it constantly in

every star, breeze, and heartbeat.
We too must live transparently and courageously.

Love, as taught in the higher knowledge, is not merely an emotion but the fundamental power of all existence.
It lives within every human being and in every atom of Creation.
To recognize love in all things is to align oneself with the source of life itself.
This recognition strengthens our spiritual energy, nourishes our consciousness, and heals the fragmentation caused by fear and ignorance.
Love is not something to search for, it is something to awaken within.

In applying these principles consistently and with awareness, one begins to transform not only themselves but also the world around them.
These teachings are not theoretical, they are lived truths that require practice, observation, and the willingness to grow.
Each day becomes a sacred classroom, and each moment, a choice between stagnation and evolution.
In choosing peace, respect, truth, and love, we become co-creators with Creation, actively shaping a better future through the might of our thoughts and actions.

Final advice.

My final advice to anyone seeking truth, peace, and fulfillment is simple but profound, begin to loosen your attachment to material wealth.
You are not defined by what you own.
You are a spiritual being, a fragment of Creation itself, and the more you focus on material gain, the more you forget your true nature.
Let your worth be measured by your inner growth, not the things you accumulate.

Start being honest with yourself.
Too often we wear masks, pretending, performing, hiding, afraid of being seen for who we truly are.
But the truth is, nothing good comes from deception.
The longer you wear the mask, the more disconnected you become from your core.
Inner peace begins when you drop the act and embrace your genuine self without fear.

Don't see others as your enemies.
Even if someone wrongs you, resist the urge to demonize them.
Every person, no matter how confused or hostile, is a reflection of a part of you.
We are all struggling through this life in our own ways.
By recognizing the shared suffering and confusion in others, you begin to dissolve hostility and open a path to healing.

Celebrate the presence of another human being.
It is no small thing to cross paths with someone on this journey.
Each encounter is a miracle, a rare and sacred chance to share, to laugh, to remember what it means to simply be.

These are the moments you will cherish, the ones that will echo in your memory long after they pass.

See in others the faces of your family.
The stranger on the street, the neighbor across the fence, the worker in the store, these people are not foreign to you.
They are your mothers, your fathers, your brothers, and your sisters in the universal family of life.
When you relate to others from this knowing, you live with more compassion and kindness.

Practice patience, especially when others do not understand you.
We all come from different experiences, and not everyone is at the same point in their journey.
Anger and frustration will only cause more division.
Instead, try to understand.
Speak with gentleness, and allow space for growth to happen, both in you and in them.

Give others the benefit of the doubt.
Life is complicated, and no story is ever just one-sided.
People have reasons for acting the way they do, even when they themselves are unaware of them.
Be generous with your understanding, and allow others the grace to explain, to grow, and even to stumble.

As spiritual beings, we are all here to learn, to experience, and to evolve together.
No one is above or below.
We are mirrors, each helping the other see what they cannot see alone.
Let your presence be a blessing to others, and allow others to bless you in return.

In the end, remember that what you do for others, you do for yourself.
What you give, you receive.
What you heal in others, you heal in yourself.
So live from truth, act from love, and walk forward with peace in your heart.
This is the path of Creation.

Final reminder: Who is Billy Meier?

That question changed my life the moment I began to truly search for the answer.

I investigated about him for well over two years and read hundreds of contact reports he shared with us while completely submerged myself in the study of the Creation Energy Teachings to realize the depth of who he really was.

I had the opportunity to meet him twice in person.

Those meetings were brief, but they left a lasting impression, quiet yet powerful, humble yet immense in presence.

I saw not just a man, but someone carrying an ancient knowing, as if the truth of many lifetimes lived in his words and gaze.

The spirit-form or Creation Energy within Billy Meier is none other than the "one" once known as Nokodemion.

This spirit-form is of extraordinary significance, not for mystical reasons, but because of the natural laws of Creation.

Nokodemion was the first human spirit-form to evolve beyond the material and half-material planes into the purely spiritual level of Arahat Athersata.

That evolutionary achievement comes with an eternal responsibility, to teach the laws and recommendations of Creation to the human beings of the universe.

This is not myth or fantasy, but a continuation of an evolutionary journey that spans billions of years.

That same spirit-form has returned again and again to Earth, taking up the role of a teacher, a guide, a bringer of truth, what we call a Prophet.

Across many lifetimes, Nokodemion incarnated as figures who shaped human civilization and thinking.

Names like Henoch, Elijah, Isaiah, Jeremiah, Mohammed and Jmmanuel, whom the world mistakenly knows as Jesus, are all previous personalities of this same spirit-form.

Even beyond the religious names, others like Socrates, Aristotle, and Mozart were also carriers of this same timeless essence.

Billy Meier is the seventh and final incarnation of this line of prophets.

The word "Prophet" has been so deeply misunderstood.

It doesn't mean a predictor of doom, nor a figure to worship.

It simply means one who brings the truth, especially the timeless truth of the Spiritual Teaching.

I witnessed this firsthand.

He does not force his knowledge onto anyone.

He simply offers it, with clarity and certainty, for those willing to listen and think for themselves.

Through my encounters with him and study of his writings, I learned that this mission is far from over.

After Billy Meier's death, Nokodemion Creation Energy will reincarnate once again in the year 2075.

This next incarnation will also carry the task of continuing the teaching, but not as a prophet.

The era of prophets will end with Billy.

The next step is teaching without the barrier of idolization, with human beings finally learning to stand in truth without dependency.

There is even a sign foretold of the next incarnation, a birthmark located exactly where Jmmanuel was stabbed during his crucifixion.

This is not to glorify suffering, but to help identify the new bearer of truth in a world that may still be skeptical.

That person will live and teach on Earth until the year 3999, after which the spirit-form will return once more to the Arahat Athersata plane to continue its own spiritual evolution.

Such a journey, spanning so many eons and lifetimes, reveals how immense and structured the path of learning truly is.

What astounds me most is how grounded it all is in the logic of Creation.

There is no mysticism or superstition here.

Everything, each law, each teaching, follows a precise order.

Evolution, not worship, is the key.
Learning, not blind faith, is the path.
And love, knowledge, peace, and inner freedom are the true goals of our existence.
Billy Meier never asked for followers, only thinkers.
He carries the Teaching, but it is up to us to live it.

Meeting him gave me a direct glimpse into what human potential looks like when aligned with Creation.
It made me realize that the truth has always been here, patiently waiting for us to mature enough to understand it.
The Creation Energy Teachings are not tied to one man, they are universal.
But they needed a clear voice to guide them into the modern world.
Billy Meier was chosen for that, not because he is special, but because his spirit-form was ready for the task.

To know Billy Meier is to recognize the path of Nokodemion, not as a story of one man, but as a reflection of what is possible for all of us.
He reminds me that we are all eternal, all evolving, and all capable of uncovering truth.
I am grateful for the brief moments I spent in his presence, and even more so for the vast knowledge he has brought forth.
In the end, he is not to be worshiped, but to be understood.
For through understanding, we become truly free.

If you choose to follow his teachings, as I have, you will come to know a peace that is no longer dependent on the state of the outside world.
Even as chaos unfolds on the surface of life, you will remain inwardly calm, stable, and free.
This peace is not a passing feeling or a hopeful illusion, it is the direct result of living according to the creational laws and recommendations that govern all existence.

From my own experience, I can say that these teachings have enabled me to access the mights of my thoughts.
I now understand that my thoughts are the origin of everything I experience.

They are not random or meaningless, but living forces that attract corresponding results.
By learning to think in line with the creational truth, I have discovered the immense creative power that resides within me, and within every human being.

This isn't merely a philosophy to admire from a distance.
It is a way of living that demands effort, honesty, and constant self-reflection.
But it is also a path that leads to real joy, clarity, and strength.
I have seen myself change, not because I forced it, but because I aligned with the truth that was always present in me and all around me.
The transformation happens from the inside out.

The teachings also bring great comfort, not through escape, but through understanding.
You come to know your eternal nature as a spirit-form that lives countless lives for the purpose of evolving.
You begin to see the deeper meaning behind your challenges, and you learn to welcome them as opportunities for growth.
Fear fades, because fear cannot survive where knowledge and truth have taken root.

Billy's mission is not to save the world but to illuminate the path so that each person can save themselves.
He points toward Creation, eternal, unmeasurable, ever-evolving, and shows how we are each a part of it, never separate.
We are meant to live in harmony with it, to understand it, and to fulfill our purpose as carriers of consciousness and evolution.

When one truly embraces this path, a new kind of human being begins to emerge, not physically different, but conscious, peaceful, and powerful from within.
This is the silent revolution of the spirit.
It is not loud, dramatic, or political.
It happens in the hearts and minds of those who have chosen truth over lies, and responsibility over blame.

This is what I have found by walking this path.

And though I am still evolving, still learning, I now live with a certainty that cannot be shaken.

I am no longer lost.

I am no longer afraid.

I am a student of truth, a child of Creation, and a conscious participant in the eternal becoming.

And that, in itself, is the greatest transformation any human can undergo.

Final Chapter.
The Creation Energy Teachings.

Within the realm of the Creation Energy Teachings, a profound and life-altering revelation patiently awaits every individual who dares to open themselves to its eternal truth.

These teachings, transmitted through the ages and now offered in their purest form by the Herald of this universe, Billy Meier, are not mere philosophical musings.

They are the embodiment of universal law, delivered with clarity for the benefit of all who seek understanding, peace, and evolution of consciousness.

When one begins to genuinely live in accordance with these principles and follow the recommendations given, not as dogma, but as a compass pointing to inner truth, something extraordinary starts to take place.

Slowly at first, then with growing clarity, the patterns of one's life begin to shift.

Like clouds parting before the sun, confusion dissolves and synchronicity arises.

You begin to understand the movements of life with greater purpose and precision.

At a certain moment in this journey, a remarkable shift occurs.

Events that once seemed random or chaotic begin to align in harmony with your thoughts, your efforts, and your inner transformation.

Opportunities emerge as if summoned.

Challenges are met with previously unseen strength.

It is not coincidence, nor is it magic, it is the natural outcome of aligning oneself with the truth of the Creation.

You may refer to these moments as miracles, for they will appear to transcend the boundaries of what you believed possible.
But in reality, they are not miracles in the mystical or religious sense.
They are evidence of the laws of cause and effect working in perfect harmony with the Creation Energy that flows through all life.
They happen not because of superstition or blind faith, but because you have begun to live in conscious accordance with universal law.

This tool of transformation, this sacred teaching, is not reserved for a select few, nor is it hidden behind rituals or hierarchy.
It is available to all who possess the courage to seek, to question, and most importantly, to act.
No matter your background, your past, or your circumstances, the Creation Energy Teachings stand before you like an open gate.
The only requirement is the willingness to walk through it with honesty, discipline, and humility.

Billy Meier, as the Herald of this universe and the final prophet of the Nokodemion lineage, has delivered this message not to control or to convert, but to offer liberation from ignorance and suffering.
His life stands as a living testimony to the truth he imparts, one born not of belief, but of experience, knowledge, and responsibility.
Those who dismiss his teachings out of prejudice or pride rob only themselves of the light that could be theirs.

To embrace these teachings is to begin the great inward journey.
It is to peel back the layers of ego, illusion, and false identity and remember who you truly are, a fragment of Creation, imbued with purpose and potential.
This remembrance brings order to chaos, healing to wounds, and clarity to confusion.
It does not promise ease, but it does promise growth, real, lasting, meaningful growth.

Let no one convince you that you are powerless.
You are not.
You are a creator within the Creation, and your thoughts, your decisions, and your intentions shape the reality around you.
With the right guidance, such as that offered through these teachings,

you can harness this power not for selfish gain, but for your own spiritual evolution and the betterment of all life around you.

So take this message seriously.
Let it settle into your thoughts and weigh heavily on your conscience, not with burden but with the gravitas it deserves.
The teachings are not a fantasy, they are a roadmap.
And when followed with sincerity and patience, they lead not to miracles, but to something far greater: the awakening of your true self and your rightful place within the infinite unfolding of Creation.

Final words.

L et humanity heed this urgent call, a call not born from fear nor fleeting emotion, but from the timeless knowing that pulses at the core of all existence.
It is the echo of ancient wisdom, the same voice that has guided the wise across millennia, now rising again to awaken our dormant memory.
It speaks to us not through thunder or fire, but through the quiet certainty of truth.
This is the message we must allow to penetrate the hardened layers of forgetfulness, and take root in the fertile ground of our inner knowing.

May this eternal message be etched deep within our hearts and minds, not as a passing inspiration, but as an enduring force of remembrance.
We must no longer live as if we are temporary visitors, disconnected from purpose and meaning.
We are not isolated sparks flickering briefly in the void.
We are flames of an eternal fire, lit by Creation itself, destined to burn brightly across the endless unfolding of time and space.
That truth must become the bedrock of our thoughts, our choices, and our lives.

We are beings of eternity, timeless travelers who have crossed the boundaries of death and birth more times than we can remember.
Before this current life, we have lived many others, wearing countless faces, walking different lands, loving and losing under many suns.
And yet, through all those lives, one constant has remained: our indestructible spirit, shaped by the laws of Creation and enriched by every experience.

And we are far from finished.
The journey continues beyond this life and will stretch far into the

unfolding future.

More lives await us, more lessons, more growth, more refinement of our essence.

The road is long, but it is not meaningless.

Each life is a sacred chapter in an infinite book, and each of us is both author and reader of our own story.

Knowing this, how can we waste even one moment in ignorance or division?

This understanding must awaken within us a sense of deep reverence for one another.

For if we are all eternal beings, then no one is truly separate.

We are strands of the same great web, unique in form yet bound together in purpose.

My soul has met yours before and shall meet it again.

What I do to you, I do to myself.

There is no stranger, only reflections of the self wearing unfamiliar masks.

Let us therefore dismantle the illusions that divide us, nationality, skin color, belief systems, wealth, and status.

These are but temporary costumes of the material world, and they dissolve like mist in the face of truth.

Beneath them lies what is real and lasting: the spiritual essence that connects all human beings as one great family.

When we begin to live with this awareness, our world will transform from the inside out.

Our interconnectedness is not just a spiritual ideal, it is a cosmic law.

Just as the stars align in sacred geometry, so too do our lives intersect according to universal patterns.

No meeting is accidental, no challenge is without meaning, no life is without value.

Everything and everyone plays a part in the grand evolution of consciousness.

When we embrace this truth, we no longer look for enemies, we look for brothers and sisters.

Let this realization guide us, not only in our personal lives but also in how we shape our societies.

Let it guide how we educate, how we govern, how we care for one another and for our planet.

We must no longer build our world on competition, exploitation, and fear, but on cooperation, balance, and truth.

This is not a dream, it is the destiny we are called to fulfill.

So let this call ring loud within us.

Let it awaken the memory of who we truly are.

We are not broken.

We are not lost.

We are eternal beings of light and wisdom, called now to rise above the illusion of separation and become once again what we were always meant to be, a unified, conscious Human race walking in harmony with Creation itself.

Final.

Life, in its deepest and most profound essence, functions very much like a grand and intricate play, one whose stage is the material world, and whose actors are each of us, clothed in temporary identities.

We enter into this world much like performers, stepping onto the stage of existence to play out roles chosen for our learning and development.

These roles vary from life to life, from scene to scene, and they are never the same.

One moment we are teachers, the next we are students.

One day we are strong and confident, the next we are fragile and uncertain.

Through each role, we are not meant to become the character, but to evolve the spirit behind it.

Every experience, every encounter with another human being, and every internal struggle we face is a carefully placed moment in this play, designed not to define us permanently, but to shape and awaken us.

The script of life is written by the impulses of our inner consciousness and the laws of Creation, which bring to us the exact lessons we need for the development of our awareness.

When one act of learning ends, we step back, rest, reflect, and prepare for the next.

This may happen over the course of a single lifetime or across many, but the rhythm of preparation, performance, and transformation is a timeless one.

Once an episode concludes, be it a stage of life, a challenge overcome, or even an entire incarnation, we return to the metaphysical changing room of existence.

There, the deeper part of us, the spirit-form, does not rest idly but instead integrates what was learned, readying itself for the next journey. This cycle of birth, experience, reflection, and rebirth is as natural as the rising and setting of the sun.

And knowing this cycle intimately, not merely as a belief but through inner observation and understanding, has forever changed the way I walk through this life.

I no longer move blindly, I walk with eyes open and spirit aware.

Sadly, many of the "actors" in this play become completely entangled in the illusion of the roles they inhabit.

They begin to believe that the mask they wear is their true face, and that the script they follow is the totality of their being.

They form deep attachments to material identities, external validation, and fleeting circumstances.

They react strongly to the drama, the arguments, the pride, the loss, mistaking them for ultimate reality.

As a result, they become trapped in cycles of confusion, suffering, and emotional turmoil.

The more they cling to the stage, the more distant they become from their true purpose.

But through the wisdom offered in the Creation Energy Teachings, I've been shown how to step back from this confusion and observe life for what it really is, a school, a stage, a sacred process.

These teachings did not merely tell me to be calm or detached, they gave me the tools to understand why things happen the way they do.

I've come to realize that I am not the actor, I am the observer who watches and learns through the acting.

I am not the suffering, I am the one evolving through the suffering.

I am not the temporary personality, I am the eternal spirit-form growing through each temporary experience.

This understanding has given me a freedom that I never thought was possible.

It has allowed me to step outside the performance and watch it with clarity, peace, and depth.

When difficulties come, I no longer curse them, I ask, What am I being shown here?

When people mistreat me, I no longer feel destroyed, I ask, What inner strength is this moment calling forth?
I now see that every joy, every pain, every relationship, and every challenge is part of a scene that is here not to defeat me, but to instruct me.

By choosing to observe rather than attach, I have freed myself from the emotional chaos that once ruled my mind.
I have learned to watch my thoughts instead of being ruled by them.
I remain centered in the knowledge that the stage of life is not a trap, it is a mirror, reflecting back to me what I must confront, heal, and ultimately transcend.
I no longer move through life trying to force outcomes or control others.
Instead, I flow with the understanding that all things serve the process of evolution, mine and everyone else's.

Each role I play, each lesson I observe, and each truth I uncover brings me closer to the core of who I really am.
I am not here merely to survive, to succeed, or to suffer, I am here to become.
To become wiser, more peaceful, more aligned with the laws of Creation.
With every act, the spirit within me grows in consciousness and clarity.
And with each passing moment, I am reminded that I am not the play,
I am the one who watches it, who learns from it, and who ultimately outgrows it.
I am a conscious, evolving being on an eternal journey back to truth, back to source, back to myself.

Back Cover

S even: The Last Book is the culmination of a journey that began with a single question, *Who am I, really?*

Through six previous books, I have explored the teachings, principles, and universal truths drawn from the Creation Energy Teachings of Billy Meier. This final volume is my most personal and complete expression, a distillation of all I've learned, lived, and remembered on the path back to the Source.

This book is not just about knowledge, it's about inner transformation. It is for those who are seeking more than answers, those who are ready for clarity, for peace, and for an unshakable connection to Creation itself. These teachings have guided me through darkness, expanded my consciousness, and revealed a reality far vaster and more beautiful than what we are taught to believe. Now, I offer them to you, from one human being to another.

In these pages, I speak directly to the part of you that already knows the truth. The words are only reminders. The real work, your true evolution, happens within. This is a book about aligning with the natural laws of life, learning to listen inwardly, and becoming conscious of the eternal energy that flows through all things. If you've made it here, it means you're ready.

I didn't write this book to be followed, I wrote it to be used. My path has been imperfect, human, and real. That's what makes the journey honest. I've asked the questions. I've wrestled with the answers. And through it all, I've come to see that Creation never hides, it simply waits for us to awaken.

Seven is not the end. It is a beginning, a bridge, a return. Walk forward with courage. The truth lives within you.

— **Waid Sainvil**

NOKODEMION